THE York*shire*
Moors and Dales

THE Yorkshire
Moors and Dales

Text by Robin Whiteman
Photographs by Rob Talbot

·SEVEN·
DIALS·

First published in 1991 by George Weidenfeld & Nicolson Ltd,

This paperback edition first published in 2000 by
Seven Dials, Cassell & Co., Wellington House,
125 Strand, London, WC2R 0BB

Distributed in the United States of America by
Sterling Publishing Co., Inc., 387 Park Avenue South,
New York, NY 10016-8810

British Library Cataloguing in Publication Data
A catalogue for this book is available from the British Library
ISBN 1 84188 080 9

Half-Title Page East Gill Force, near Keld, located by a wooden footbridge on a tributary of the Swale. The
remote, former lead-mining village of Keld, 1100 feet above sea level, lies amidst wild crags and bleak
moorland, almost at the head of Swaledale, in an area where there is an impressive collection of waterfalls,
including the dramatic Kisdon Force. The Pennine Way, the long-distance footpath, passes within a few
hundred yards of the village (which has a Youth Hostel, formerly a shooting lodge).

Title Page White Scars – a limestone plateau on the western flanks of Ingleborough – with Whernside, the
highest mountain in Yorkshire, in the distance. The limestone blocks, making up the pavement top, are
called 'clints', while the fissures, formed by the dissolving action of rainwater on surface cracks, are known
as 'grykes'. Six hundred feet below the limestone pavement at White Scars is White Scar Cave, a show
cave discovered in 1923 and opened to the public four years later.

Contents

ACKNOWLEDGMENTS

Robin Whiteman and Rob Talbot would particularly like to acknowledge English Heritage's generous co-operation in allowing them to take photographs of their numerous properties in the North Region. They are also extremely grateful to the following: Castle Howard Estate Ltd and the Hon. Simon Howard; The Trustees of the Chatsworth Settlement, Yorkshire Estate, Bolton Abbey; Kilnsey Park; Whitby Gazette, Yorkshire Regional Newspapers Ltd; and the various National Park Information Offices scattered throughout the Moors and the Dales. Special thanks go to Trisha for her assistance with the research; Sheila for her support; and not forgetting George, a border collie, almost human and good company. Appreciation goes also to all those individuals and organisations too numerous to mention by name who nevertheless made such a valuable contribution. Last, but not least, a special acknowledgment is due to Colin Grant at Weidenfeld & Nicolson.

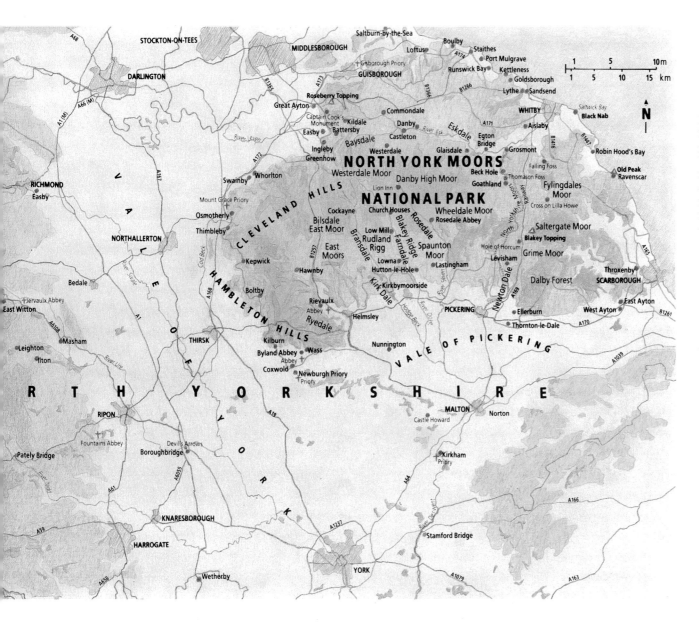

Map of the Yorkshire Moors and Dales showing the location of places illustrated in this book. The borders of the National Parks are indicated by a green line, abbeys and churches by a red cross, hills or peaks by a red triangle, and other places of interest, including castles and waterfalls, by a red dot.

INTRODUCTION

**ASKRIGG
WENSLEYDALE**

On the north side of the River Ure,
mid-way between Aysgarth and
Hawes, the grey-stone village of
Askrigg lies in the shelter of
Ellerkin Scar and Askrigg
Common. The market, which was
granted a charter in 1587, declined
when the Richmond-Lancaster
turnpike road – authorized in 1751
– was re-routed through Hawes.
Most of the present buildings date
from the eighteenth and nineteenth
centuries, when Askrigg became
prosperous through industries such
as clock-making, textiles and hand-
knitting. The Church of St Oswald,
near the market cross, dates from
the thirteenth century and has a
fifteenth-century tower. The village
was used by the BBC for filming
the popular television series *All
Creatures Great and Small*: it became
'Darrowby', and Cringley House
(now called Skeldale House), on
the market square, became the
surgery-home of the country vet
James Herriot. The flat-topped hill
in the photograph is Addlebrough,
1,562 feet above sea level.

From the seaside resort of Scarborough and the fishing village of Staithes the North York Moors National Park stretches westward for some 35 miles – across wild, heather moorland and deep secluded dales – to the wind-swept heights of Roseberry Topping and the Cleveland Hills. From the historic city of York, where ancient Britons, Romans, Saxons, Vikings and Normans fought and lived and died, the Vale of York runs north-west – past the magnificent ruins of the medieval abbey of Fountains – and on towards the bustling market town of Richmond, with its rocky fortress guarding the valley of the River Swale. From Swaledale, Coverdale, Wensleydale and Wharfedale, the Yorkshire Dales National Park reaches westward for a further 35 miles – across limestone hills, steep-sided valleys and a living patchwork of fields, across rivers and streams and gushing waterfalls – to the Pennines, the 'backbone' of northern England, and the western dales.

Within this unique, unspoilt area of North Yorkshire, covering almost 2,000 square miles, there is an incredible variety of scenery. On the east coast, exposed to the ever-changing moods of the North Sea, there are high, vertical cliffs, sandy, wave-swept beaches and dark, secluded bays. Within the two National Parks, there are rich green valleys, uninterrupted expanses of high moorland, peaceful oases of dappled woodland, and rugged peaks with deep, dramatic ravines.

But, however diverse the scenery, the region has far more to offer than landscape, magical though it is. Hidden within the folds of the hills, or perched high upon a rocky cliff, or set gem-like in an emerald plain, there are thriving towns like Richmond, Ripon and Whitby; enchanting villages like Helmsley, Robin Hood's Bay, Hutton-le-Hole and Thornton-le-Dale; ancient castles like those at Skipton, Pickering and Scarborough; glorious abbeys like Rievaulx and Byland; stately mansions like Castle Howard; and then – to crown them all – there is York, a medieval city, steeped in history and famous throughout the world for its rich and varied heritage.

Since early man roamed and hunted the primeval forests and swamps of the Yorkshire Moors and Dales, the character, life and traditions of its people have helped to shape and mould the landscape. From the prehistoric stone circle at Yockenthwaite to the modern radomes of Fylingdales, the region contains a wealth of monuments and buildings – all with their own captivating story to tell and history to reveal.

The North York Moors

Close to the junction of the Hutton-le-Hole, Rosedale, Westerdale and Castleton roads, 1,409 feet above sea level, is the 9-foot-high, Young Ralph Cross. The stone cross, which replaced the original wooden cross, was broken into three sections in 1961. From Old Ralph Cross, a quarter of a mile to the west at 1,420 feet, the North Sea and the prominent landmark of Roseberry Topping can be clearly seen. A short distance south of Young Ralph Cross is a memorial to the archaeologist and naturalist Frank Elgee (1880–1944), which was unveiled in 1953. The remote Lion Inn, about a mile south on Blakey Ridge, often gets cut off by snow in winter. It was formerly an ale-house, used by pannier traffic carrying moorland coal from the Blakey pits to the lime works at Hutton-le-Hole.

High on the moors near the head of Rosedale, not far north of the remote Lion Inn at Blakey, stands a remarkable group of marker stones and crosses known as Old Ralph, Young Ralph, Fat Betty and the Margery Stone. Like many of the hundreds of similar stones found scattered throughout the region, their origins are shrouded in mystery. The oldest is probably Lilla Cross on Fylingdales Moor, which is thought to date from the early seventh century. To account for their presence in the landscape, many of the stones are associated with stories and legends. The group near Rosedale Head are no exception.

Old Ralph is said to have been a lay servant at the small Cistercian nunnery at Rosedale, founded some time before 1158. By the end of the century a sister convent had been founded, some 9 miles to the north-west at Baysdale. Separated by an inhospitable tract of high, wild moorland, the communities lived in relative isolation. In addition to his normal duties, Ralph served as a moorland guide. One day he set out to escort Sister Elizabeth of Rosedale to a point midway between the two convents, where she had arranged to meet Sister Margery of Baysdale to try and settle a boundary dispute. A thick, chilling sea fog (known locally as a roak) suddenly descended and the parties became lost. Ralph told the nun to wait beside a large stone while he set out to find Sister Margery. Elizabeth knelt and prayed, maintaining her cold and lonely vigil for hours. Eventually the roak lifted, and, by climbing on top of the stone, she could see both Ralph and Margery, standing at two separate stones, only a few hundred yards away. Ralph is reputed to have marked the position of each stone and given them names: the White Cross after Sister Elizabeth's white robes, although it later became known as Fat Betty; the Margery Stone, sometimes called Old Margery, or Margery Bradley, after the Baysdale nun; and Old Ralph after himself. Young Ralph is a more recent arrival, probably erected in the eighteenth century near the site of an earlier cross called 'Crux Radulphi', which is known to have served as a boundary stone in the thirteenth century.

Young Ralph also has a story. It is said that the cross was erected by a local farmer – at the spot where a poor traveller had died from exhaustion – not only to act as a guide for travellers crossing the moors, but also to provide a means for their sustenance. At the top of the tall and slender cross is a hollow in which, according to an old custom, those who could afford it should place money or food to help others in need. The cross has been damaged twice: first in 1961 by a man attempting to reach the hollow; and again in 1984 by vandals. Each time it has been carefully repaired.

Young Ralph's Cross stands at the geological centre of the North York Moors and at the junction of a number of ancient ridgeways. It is sited on the west side of the Castleton to Hutton-le-Hole road, close to the meeting-point of roads from Rosedale, Eskdale, Westerdale and Farndale. At over 1,400 feet above sea level, this elevated route across the open moors is often impassable in winter because of snow. Yet, if visibility is good, the 9-foot-high cross can be seen for miles around. Young Ralph, however, has become much more than a landmark, for in 1974 it was adopted as the emblem of the North York Moors National Park.

Designated in 1952 and covering an area of over 553 square miles, the park is bounded to the east by the North Sea, and to the north, west and south by a horseshoe of lowland plains, including the Cleveland Plain and the Vales of York, Mowbray and Pickering. The escarpments of the Cleveland and Hambleton Hills form the northern and western boundaries, rising steeply to nearly 1,000 feet before sweeping eastward for some 35 miles to end with the high, rugged cliffs of the Yorkshire coast.

The rocks of the North York Moors belong entirely to the Jurassic period, formed by sediment laid down horizontally on the bed of a tropical sea over 140 million years ago. Cataclysmic movements in the earth's crust forced the sea bed upwards while tilting it towards the south. Comprised of shales, sandstones and limestones, the hills were shaped and moulded by the erosive effect of numerous, and sometimes dramatic, changes of climate spanning millions of years. Glacial action smoothed the surface of the hills, deepened the valleys and deposited clay, boulders and stones, But the present moorland landscape was not formed entirely by natural forces. In part, it was created by man.

WESTERDALE MOOR

Nearly half of the North York Moors National Park consists of wide expanses of open heather moorland, blossoming in August and September and grazed by sheep throughout the year. It is the largest area of heather-covered upland in England and is managed by controlled burning. Each year, between November and March when the peat is damp, the farmers and gamekeepers periodically set light to patches of old woody heather in order to encourage new growth. Known locally as 'swiddening', controlled burning does not generate the enormous heat of accidental fires and, therefore, the peat and the roots of the heather are not destroyed. The new green shoots provide essential nourishment for both sheep and grouse. Throughout the central moors are lines of shooting butts, built of stone and covered with heather or bilberries to blend in with the surrounding landscape. They are used to screen the shooters during the grouse-shooting season: from 12 August to 10 December.

Whitby
and the Yorkshire Coast

Black Nab, the dark sinister headland at the eastern end of Saltwick Bay, was extensively quarried for alum in the seventeenth and eighteenth centuries. On the nearby cliff top, are the Whitby High Lighthouse, built in 1857–8, and the Fog Signal Station, which occupies the site of the Low Lighthouse, demolished in the 1890s. The High light is 240 feet above sea level and has a beam of 22 miles. Known locally as the Hawsker Bull, the siren sounds four times every 90 seconds in foggy weather and can be heard 10 miles out to sea. Access to the small sandy beach of Saltwick Bay can be gained by a steep track leading down from the caravan site at the top of the cliff. Seven-and-a-half acres of cliff land, including Saltwick Nab, belong to the National Trust.

Man has exploited the rocks and minerals of the North York Moors since time immemorial. The stone was used by the people of the Bronze Age to build cairns, circles and barrows, as well as enclosure walls and houses. Ironstone has been mined and worked for over 2,000 years, from the Iron Age until 1964, when the last mine closed at North Skelton in Cleveland, north-east of Guisborough. Sandstone has been quarried for building material, volcanic 'whinstone' for road construction, boulder clay for brick manufacture, and limestone (after processing) for use in agriculture and industry. Coal was extracted from mines in commercially viable amounts during the eighteenth and nineteenth centuries. One of the largest moorland collieries was at Castleton, which, at its peak in 1817, employed about fifty miners.

A hard variety of coal, or lignite – found throughout the moors, but particularly on the coast – has been zealously sought after for centuries: a valuable glossy, black fossilized wood called Whitby jet, which can be carved and polished to make jewellery and ornaments. Although small delicately worked articles of jet have been found on Bronze Age burial sites, the earliest reference to jet working in Whitby is an entry, dated 1394, in the account rolls of the Benedictine abbey. Bede, describing Britain in the eighth century, wrote: 'It has much and excellent jet, which is black and sparkling, glittering at the fire, and when heated, drives away serpents; being warmed with rubbing, it holds fast whatever is applied to it, like amber.' Jet's power to attract objects when rubbed has been remarked on by numerous writers down the ages. It came to be valued for its magical properties and was used to make charms and amulets to ward off the evil eye; when ground into a powder and added to medicines, it was also thought to possess the power of healing. Excavations at the Roman signal station at Goldsborough, near Kettleness, have revealed a number of jet ornaments, including two rings. Ancient artifacts of Whitby jet have been found not only throughout Britain, but even as far away as the Middle East.

Until the early nineteenth century jet had always been fashioned by primitive means, using a knife, file and rubbing stone. The first mechanized working of jet at Whitby began in a tentative way with the turning of beads. By 1870, after Queen Victoria had made the stone fashionable by introducing it into court circles, some 1,400 men and boys were employed in extracting and carving the jet. Shortly afterwards, the industry went into a decline. Today, only a few people in Whitby are engaged in the production of jet jewellery.

Alum, a chemical used in the tanning and dyeing industries, was first quarried at Slape-wath, near Guisborough in 1604. By the middle of the eighteenth century the region had become the major producer of alum in Britain, with many of the quarries sited along the coast. In the nineteenth century the development of a cheap process of producing alum by treating colliery waste with sulphuric acid led to the collapse of the industry in north-east Yorkshire. The last works to close were at Boulby, near Loftus, in 1871. The scars of abandoned alum workings are particularly evident along the coast at Ravenscar, Sandsend, Kettleness, Saltwick Nab near Whitby, and Stoupe Brow near Robin Hood's Bay.

Potash deposits were discovered at Aislaby, near Whitby, in 1939. Further explorations for potash revealed a workable seam near Staithes and in 1969 work started on building Britain's first potash mine and refinery at Boulby, within the National Park. Since 1981 the mine has also produced salt, most of which is used by local authorities for de-icing roads in winter.

Many villages and hamlets in the North York Moors were established or substantially enlarged by mining activity in the region. Those most dramatically affected were the tiny fishing villages and ports along the coast, where extensive quarrying of the cliffs has been carried out for nearly 400 years. Port Mulgrave, for example, was developed in the 1850s as a major outlet for ironstone from the nearby Grinkle mine. By 1916 the port was abandoned and allowed to fall into decay. The outer sea wall has now been washed away and the harbour has almost silted up.

Whitby, at the mouth of the River Esk, grew and prospered in the seventeenth and eighteenth centuries when alum was shipped out of the port. Between 1753 and 1837 Whitby was involved in whaling, sending in its heyday twenty ships in one season to the icy Arctic waters. In 1794 it was one of the country's leading seaports building twenty-five ships a year. The great explorer and navigator Captain James Cook moved to the town in 1746, and it was in Whitby-built ships that he sailed on his epic voyages of discovery.

EAST HARBOUR SCARBOROUGH

Harald Hardrada, King of Norway, and Tostig, brother of the Saxon King Harold, landed at Scarborough in 1066, before the battle of Stamford Bridge, and sacked the town. Scarborough is not mentioned in the Domesday survey of 1086 and the earliest record of the place-name occurs in 1158, as *Scardeburg*. There are two alternative meanings: 'the fort of Skarthi' (an Old Norse personal name meaning 'hare-lipped') or 'the hill by a gap'. The 'gap' refers to the valley through which the town is approached from the south. The discovery of medicinal springs in the seventeenth century led to the development of the town as a spa. Its popularity increased, and today it is one of the largest east-coast resorts in Britain. Anne Brontë, who died in 1849, is buried in St Mary's churchyard below the castle.

ST OSWALD'S CHURCH LYTHE

Standing high on the cliff top above Sandsend and to the east of the village of Lythe, the parish church of St Oswald was essentially rebuilt in 1910. During the partial demolition of the original building, a number of carved stones were discovered, dating from the ninth and tenth centuries. These Anglo-Saxon and Anglo-Danish fragments, including cross-heads and hog-back gravestones, are on display in the spacious crypt of the church. One of the former priests of Lythe was Cardinal John Fisher, who was executed for treason on Tower Hill, London, in 1535. The church contains a number of memorials to the Phipps, who were Earls and Lords of nearby Mulgrave Castle in the eighteenth and nineteenth centuries. Now the home of the Marquis of Normanby, their castellated mansion stands to the south of the church. In Mulgrave Woods are the remains of Old Mulgrave Castle, said to have been occupied by the legendary giant Wade.

WHITBY ABBEY

High on the cliffs, overlooking the old whaling port and the mouth of the River Esk, stand the sandstone ruins of Whitby Abbey. It was first founded in AD 657, for both men and women, by St Hilda. Within her lifetime the monastery became not only a great centre of learning, but also the home of Caedmon, the celebrated poet mentioned by Bede. At the top of the 199 steps which lead to the abbey is a 20-foot-high cross dedicated to Caedmon, who died in AD 680. Its design is based on the Ruthwell Cross and was unveiled on 21 September 1898 by Alfred Austin, the Poet Laureate. The monastery was destroyed by the Danes in AD 867. It was refounded as a Benedictine priory in about 1077 by William de Percy and dedicated to St Peter and St Hilda. The present remains are essentially thirteenth century. But how and when it became an abbey is unknown.

WHITBY ABBEY AND ST MARY'S CHURCH WHITBY

Standing on the wind-swept heights of East Cliff, the possible site of a Roman coastal signal station, the distinctive ruins of Whitby Abbey remain as an aid to navigation. According to Bede, *Streaneshalch*, the Anglo-Saxon name for Whitby, means *fari sinus*, or the 'haven of the watch-tower'. The abbey was dissolved in 1539, and all that survives today is essentially the roofless shell of the church. The western range is now occupied by the Victorian-fronted Abbey House. Close by the abbey is the parish church of St Mary, dating from the early twelfth century. Inside is a fascinating arrangement of box pews, galleries and balconies, including the early seventeenth century Cholmley Pew with its white barley-sugar columns. The eye-catching three-decker pulpit dates from 1778 and was moved to its present position in 1847.

WHITBY HARBOUR

The ancient fishing port of Whitby, surrounded on three sides by the moors and on the fourth by the North Sea, is rich in legends, hauntings and superstitions. Bram Stoker's blood-thirsty vampire, Dracula, allegedly arrived at Whitby in the shape of a large black dog: a Russian schooner, with a corpse lashed to the wheel, is driven aground in a storm and the creature is seen to leap ashore and head for St Mary's graveyard. Although he frequented the cemetery, and some maintain was buried there, Dracula was destroyed in Transylvania. The idea of the supernatural dog may have been derived from the local tradition of a demon called the Barguest. This terrifying creature, which took the form of a monstrous hound with glowing red eyes, was said to have stalked the narrow streets and alleys at night. It was feared as a harbinger of death.

SANDSEND AND WHITBY
from Lythe Bank

Sandsend is a village of inns, cottages and hotels, resting at the foot of Lythe Bank, and at the north-western end of the long sandy beach of Sandsend Wyke. From the remains of Old Mulgrave Castle, deep in the heart of Mulgrave Woods, two streams run parallel to each other to divide the village into two before entering the sea. At the Whitby end of the village is East Row, overlooking East Row Beck, while Sandsend itself, with its small nineteenth-century church, stretches up both sides of Sandsend Beck. Sandsend Ness, to the north, is scarred with the remains of alum quarries. The distant harbour in the photograph is Whitby. It was there that the gifted Frank Meadow Sutcliffe, who was born in Leeds in 1853, came to live in his late teens. He is famed for his atmospheric photographs portraying life in the fishing community of Whitby at the beginning of the twentieth century.

SALTWICK BAY

The low rocky point of Saltwick Nab lies one mile to the east of Whitby, and is reached from East Cliff by a cliff-top path, which forms part of the 108-mile-long Cleveland Way. Officially opened in May 1969, the long distance footpath starts at the market town of Helmsley, in the southern Moors, and finishes at Filey, some 7 miles south-east of Scarborough. From Saltburn to the thin, pointed headland of Filey Brig, it follows the coast for over 50 miles. Originally an ancient trackway, the route traverses Boulby Cliff, near Staithes, which, at 666 feet above sea level, is the highest cliff on England's east coast. The Yorkshire coastline is notorious for storms, and literally thousands of ships have been lost on the rocks over the years. The wrecks at Saltwick Bay include the *Rohilla*, a Red Cross hospital ship of 7,409 tons belonging to the British India Steam Navigation Company, which smashed onto a reef near Saltwick Nab on 29 October 1914.

STAITHES

Derived from the Old English word *staeth*, meaning 'landing place', Staithes once served as a landing place for nearby Seaton. The oldest part of Staithes lies at the foot of Cowbar Nab on the banks of Staithes or Roxby Beck. Although the village has a harbour protected by breakwaters, many of the fishermen moor their cobles in the sheltered mouth of the beck. The flat-bottomed, clinker-built coble, the traditional fishing boat of the area, is designed to be launched bow first on the open beach, even in raging surf. From Bank Top to the harbour wall, the tightly packed cottages spill down the steep cliff side, fitting into the slopes wherever space allows. The roofs are a mixture of warm red pantiles and cold grey slate, streaked with the white guano of generations of shrieking seagulls. Thirteen cottages were swept away in 1745, including the shop where James Cook was an apprentice.

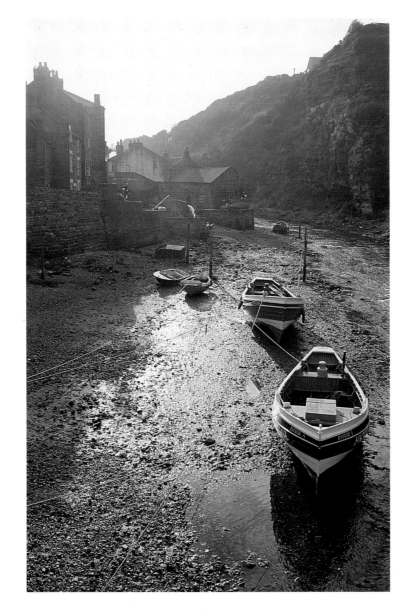

PORT MULGRAVE

Lying between Staithes and Runswick Bay, the tiny hamlet of Port Mulgrave was created in the middle of the nineteenth century, when the specially constructed harbour became an outlet for the local ironstone mining industry. The rich ore from the Grinkle mines, 2 miles away, was transported by narrow-gauge railway, through three tunnels, to emerge from the bottom of the cliff at Port Mulgrave, where it was loaded onto waiting ships. Today the long-abandoned harbour is decaying, but the miners' and harbour workers' houses remain. Proposals to restore the harbour were abandoned because of its relatively isolated and inaccessible position. The cliff face was deemed unstable and with a steep descent of about 300 feet from the cliff top there were no facilities for landing a catch of any size. Thirty-eight acres of cliff and undercliff, including the bay's northern headland, now belong to the National Trust.

RUNSWICK BAY

In the spring of 1682 the entire fishing village of Runswick Bay, with the exception of one house, slipped into the sea. The village was rebuilt, but because of the unstable nature of the cliffs the land continued to slide. To prevent further erosion, a sea wall was constructed in 1970. Perched precariously on the cliff sides, the red-pantiled houses, with their tiny gardens, huddle in the shelter of Lingrow Knowle at the north-western side of the wide sandy bay. The Thatched Cottage, formerly the coastguard's house, is now a grace-and-favour residence belonging to the Marquis of Normanby. Jet mines were opened at the foot of the cliffs on the east side of the bay in the nineteenth century. The caves, known as Hob Holes, were reputed to be the haunt of a hobgoblin who could cure whooping cough. The distant headland in the photograph is Kettle Ness.

KETTLENESS

Once a thriving mining community, a large part of the cliff-top hamlet of Kettleness slid into the sea on the night of 17 December 1829. All that exists today are a few cottages and farms, a coastguard station and the Victorian railway station. Before the Whitby-to-Middlesbrough railway line could be opened in 1883, five tunnels had to be bored through the cliff between Sandsend and Kettleness. The line has now been dismantled. Much of the crumbling headland was removed by alum quarrying, which ceased in the latter half of the nineteenth century. Ironstone was also mined nearby. Excavation of the site of the nearby Roman signal station at Goldsborough unearthed the bones of a man with the skeleton of a large dog beside him, its paws on his shoulders and its head at his throat. The area is rich in fossils.

ROBIN HOOD'S BAY

With its tightly packed, red-pantiled houses descending higgledy-piggledy from the cliff top to the very edge of the North Sea, Robin Hood's Bay is a warren of steep alleyways and narrow passages. Once a notorious haven for smugglers, it is claimed that the contraband could be passed from one end of the village to the other without once appearing in the open. There are a number of blocked-up tunnel entrances in King's Beck which are thought to have been used by the smugglers. Until the end of the nineteenth century, Bay Town, to give it its local name, was a thriving fishing village. The lack of a harbour, however, meant that the size of boat was severely limited and as a port the village declined. Today the fishing boats, or cobles, are towed in and out of the sea on tractor-drawn trailers.

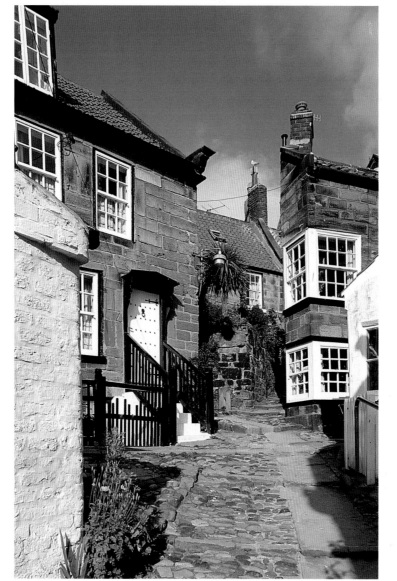

THE OPENINGS
ROBIN HOOD'S BAY

The oldest part of Bay Town, or simply Bay, lies at the foot of New Road, the steep main street leading down to the sea. Increased wealth from the fishing industry, together with the coming of the railway in 1885, led to further development higher up the slopes. Most of the present buildings date from the beginning of the eighteenth century. In 1780 the top part of King's Street, the original main street, collapsed when the cliff gave way. Over the years, nearly 200 cottages have been washed into the sea. To prevent further erosion, a seawall, 500 feet long and 40 feet high, was constructed in 1975. Numerous ships have been wrecked along the coast. In 1893, it is said, the bowsprit of a ship called *The Romulus* was driven through the window of the Bay Hotel.

OLD PEAK

Rising 600 feet above sea level, the windswept headland of Old Peak, or South Cheek, lies at the south-eastern tip of Robin Hood's Bay. Between 1640 and 1862 the cliff face was extensively quarried for alum. The Romans built a coastal signal station at the top of the cliff, the site of which is now occupied by the eighteenth-century Raven Hall Hotel. Nearby, the small hamlet of Ravenscar, with its overgrown roads, is all that remains of 'the town that never was'. At the end of the nineteenth century, ambitious plans were put forward to turn the area into a new holiday resort to rival Scarborough. Designed with the railway line from Whitby to Scarborough as its core, the proposed cliff-top town failed to attract buyers and the company went bankrupt. Ravenscar is the finishing point of the 40-mile Lyke Wake Walk.

SOUTH BAY SCARBOROUGH

The immensely popular seaside resort of Scarborough boasts two curving sandy bays, separated from each other by the headland of Castle Hill. It is on this rocky prominence that excavations have unearthed evidence of early Iron Age occupation, including weapons, tools, jewellery, a ring of jet and the remains of wattle-and-daub huts. In Roman times the hill became the site of a coastal signal station, one of a chain of similar stations set up along the coast to give warning of the approach of enemy ships. The Norman castle dates from the twelfth century (probably erected during the turbulent reign of Stephen) and became a royal stronghold under Henry II. The castle underwent many sieges, was briefly captured by Sir Thomas Stafford in 1557 and was severely damaged by the Parliamentarians during the Civil War. Shell-fire during the First World War inflicted further damage.

Guisborough
and the Northern Moors

GISBOROUGH PRIORY

Since 1974 the busy market town of Guisborough has been part of the county of Cleveland. It lies beneath the wooded northern slopes of the Cleveland Hills and is noted for its wide, tree-lined main street, cobbled verges, old houses, market cross and fifteenth-century church. Although recorded in the Domesday Book as 'Chigesburg', Guisborough probably grew up by the gates of the Augustinian priory founded in 1119 by Robert de Brus, a powerful Yorkshire baron. It was a rich foundation and in subsequent years received many donations from generous patrons, large and small. The church was destroyed by fire in 1289 and immediately rebuilt. After the Dissolution, the richly carved Bruce (or Brus) Cenotaph, an early sixteenth-century chest tomb, was placed in the nearby church of St Nicholas. The principal remains of the priory are the late thirteenth-century east end of the church, with a 56-foot arch, and the twelfth-century gatehouse and octagonal dovecote. It is in the care of English Heritage.

The earliest reference to the North York Moors is in the Venerable Bede's *Ecclesiastical History of the English Nation*, completed in AD 731. Originally called Blackamoor, meaning 'black hill moor', the region is described as 'high and remote hills, which seemed more suitable for the dens of robbers and haunts of wild beasts than for human habitation', Yet, despite its reputation for being an inhospitable wilderness, Bede mentions the founding of monasteries at Lastingham in AD 654, Whitby in 657, and Hackness, near Scarborough, some time before 680.

The moors, of course, were inhabited long before the seventh century AD, long before the arrival of the Anglo-Saxons and the Romans, and long before the arrival of the prehistoric metal-workers of the Bronze and Iron Ages. Although there is abundant evidence of ancient man's presence in the moorland landscape, the earliest buildings to survive – even if only as ruins – are castles, monasteries and churches, dating primarily from the medieval period. Among the castles of note are those at Danby and Whorlton in the north, Pickering and Helmsley in the south, and Scarborough on the coast. The best-preserved monastery is Rievaulx Abbey, but there are important remains of religious houses at Guisborough, Osmotherley (Mount Grace Priory), Byland and Whitby. Two churches of particular significance are St Mary's at Lastingham, built in 1078 on the site of the Celtic monastery mentioned by Bede, and St Gregory's Minster at Kirkdale, dating from Anglo-Saxon times.

One fortified dwelling, unique to all the counties along the Scottish and English border, is the pele tower or tower-house. These strong defensive structures, dating from the fourteenth and fifteenth centuries, were erected by the wealthier landowners to protect their animals and families from frequent incursions into the region by Scottish raiders. A few of these fortified houses still survive in the Dales and in the Vale of York. But there is one curiously isolated example in the North York Moors at West Ayton, 4 miles south-west of Scarborough – the ruined Ayton Castle, on the west bank of the River Derwent.

Yet, despite the presence of strategic fortresses and religious buildings, it is the small towns, villages and farms which best exemplify the architectural character of the region. The Domesday Survey establishes that in 1086 most of the settlements were located in the valleys and dales around the perimeter of the high moors, with scattered holdings in

Danby Dale, Eskdale, Kildale, Ryedale and Newton Dale. The people at this time were essentially farmers, whose existence depended on the plough and the cultivation of cereals. Over the next few hundred years, as the population increased, settlements moved further up the dales and up the moorsides. The thinner soils led to a shift of emphasis from arable to pastoral farming, and new markets began to develop in meat, wool, hides and other animal products. From the twelfth century until the Dissolution, at least one third of the moorland was monastic land used essentially for grazing. The nobility, however, reserved some areas of moorland exclusively for hunting, such as the Royal Forest of Pickering, an area of scattered woodland which once stretched across the Tabular Hills from Helmsley to the Derwent Valley, and as far north, perhaps, as Goathland.

Although the monastic farmers grew extremely wealthy on the international wool trade – evidence of which can be seen in the magnificence of their abbeys – the region was generally much poorer than sheep-rearing areas further south. The parish churches, for example, which had to serve numerous scattered farmsteads and hamlets over a wide area, seldom received the generous patronage characteristic of 'wool' churches in, say, the Cotswolds or East Anglia.

After the Dissolution in 1536, most of the monastic granges passed into the hands of large landowners who, over succeeding centuries, often sold parts of their estates to independent smallholders. Once they had managed to acquire freehold or leased land, these comparatively new 'yeoman' farmers prospered to the extent that they were able to replace their simple wooden houses and cottages with more durable, stone-built farmhouses, many of which still survive today.

Dating from the late seventeenth century onwards, most of these farmhouses were longhouses, designed to accommodate both family and cattle at different ends of one long, single-storeyed building with a common entrance in the middle. Although, in time, they were rebuilt, heightened and extended, the earliest longhouses were thatched, with internal 'cruck' trusses (upright timbers, often curved, secured together at the apex to form an 'A' frame). The stone blocks used for the walls mirror the geology of the region, with buff-coloured sandstones predominant in the north and grey-white limestones in the south. Pantiles were introduced for roofing material from the mid-eighteenth century and slate in the nineteenth. Many re-erected traditional buildings, including a medieval longhouse, can be seen at the Ryedale Folk Museum, Hutton-le-Hole.

CAPTAIN COOK'S MONUMENT EASBY MOOR

Captain Cook's Monument stands on the 1,064-foot-high summit of Easby Moor. Overlooking 'Captain Cook's Country' – stretching from the River Tees to Whitby – the 60-foot obelisk was erected in 1827. James Cook, the son of a farm labourer, was born on 27 October 1728 at the hamlet of Marton in Cleveland. In 1736 the family moved to Aireyholme Farm, Great Ayton. His father's employer, Thomas Skottowe, Lord of the Manor, paid for James to attend school in the village and in 1745, found him a job at Staithes as an apprentice grocer and haberdasher. The following year, at the age of eighteen, he went to Whitby where he learned his trade as a merchant seaman. He joined the Royal Navy in 1755 and spent much of the next twelve years charting the coasts of Canada and Newfoundland. He was killed on his third voyage of discovery, on 14 February 1779, at Kealakekua Bay, Hawaii.

ROSEBERRY TOPPING

The north-western corner of the
North York Moors is dominated by
the isolated hill of Roseberry
Topping, with its distinctive
pinnacle, rising 1,051 feet above sea
level. About a mile north-east of
Great Ayton and towering above
the hamlet of Newton under
Roseberry, the hill was regarded by
the Danes as sacred, the abode of
the Norse god, Odin. In 1588 it was
used as a beacon station to warn of
the approach of the Spanish
Armada, and until the seventeenth
century was called 'Osburye
Toppyne'. Its original conical
shape has been considerably
altered because of extensive mining
and quarrying activity during the
nineteenth century, when large
quantities of ironstone and the
volcanic 'whinstone' were removed.
Alum, jet, sandstone and coal have
also been removed from the hill.
From the summit there are
panoramic views over the
Cleveland Hills and across
Teesside to the North Sea. The
Topping was acquired by the
National Trust
in 1985.

QUAKERS' TROD
NEAR COMMONDALE

During the Middle Ages there was
a vast network of tracks stretching
for many hundreds of miles
throughout the Moors. These
routes, known variously as
causeways, trods, paths and ways,
were essential to the whole
economy of the region. Although
some may have prehistoric origins,
many were established by the
medieval monks to provide a firm
dry-shod route across the marshy
ground. Some of these monastic
routes, linking abbeys to their
outlying granges, can still be
traced, such as the 20-mile
causeway between Gisborough
Priory and Rosedale Abbey. The
main trade was wool and by the
end of the thirteenth century some
70,000 fleeces were produced each
year on the Moors. The wool was
transported overland by packhorse
trains to Whitby or York and from
there it was shipped to European
markets. The cleared causeway in
the photograph leads from
Commondale east towards White
Cross.

ALL SAINT'S CHURCH
GREAT AYTON

James Cook and his family moved to Aireyholme Farm, to the east of Great Ayton, in 1736. He attended school in the village, but the building was rebuilt in 1785. It has now been converted into a Captain Cook Museum. The Easby Lane cottage, thought to have been occupied by his father and mother and dated 1755, was dismantled in 1934 and shipped to Australia, where it was re-erected in the Fitzroy Gardens, Melbourne. The original site of the house is marked by a granite obelisk, hewn from Cape Everard, near Point Hicks – the first place in Australia to be sighted from Cook's *Endeavour* on 20 April 1770. As a boy, Cook would have attended services in the Norman parish church of All Saints, Great Ayton. It was altered in the eighteenth century and its west tower was pulled down in about 1880. Cook's mother and his former benefactor, Thomas Skottowe, are buried in the churchyard.

KILDALE

Recorded as 'Childale' in the Domesday Book, Kildale is a small village lying at the north-western extremity of the National Park, some 4 miles south of Guisborough. The church of St Cuthbert, near the Esk Valley railway station, was built in 1868 by Fowler Jones of York. Immediately west of the church are the earthwork remains of a Norman motte-and-bailey castle, which have been partially destroyed by the railway. The River Leven, which flows past the village, rises high on Warren Moor, in the Cleveland Hills, and meanders in a westerly direction across the Cleveland Plain to enter the Tees near Yarm. Across Kildale Moor, in Baysdale, was a Cistercian nunnery founded in about 1189 by Guido de Bovingcourt. The site is now occupied by a house. Further down the valley, at a ford of the Baysdale Beck, is a popular picnic spot, known as Hob Hole.

WHORLTON CASTLE
NEAR SWAINBY

On the north-western edge of the
Moors near the village of Swainby
lie the isolated ruins of Whorlton
Castle, dating from around the
beginning of the thirteenth century.
Built on a strategic site,
overlooking the Cleveland Plain
and at the entrance to Scugdale, it
replaced an earlier castle of the
Norman motte-and-bailey type. By
1343 the fortress was in a ruinous
state, but plans to modernize the
building led to the construction of
the late fourteenth-century
gatehouse, bearing the family coats
of arms of the Meynells, Darcys
and Grays. Much of the castle was
destroyed by the Parliamentarians
during the Civil War. The village of
Whorlton, or 'Wirueltune', was
mentioned in the Domesday survey
of 1086. During the fourteenth
century most of the inhabitants
were wiped out by plague and
today nothing remains of the
ancient village, except the roofless
ruins of the Norman church of Holy
Cross. The chancel, however, has
been preserved and is still, at
certain times of the year, used as a
place of worship.

MOUNT GRACE PRIORY
NEAR OSMOTHERLY

The Carthusians, who were the
strictest and most austere of all the
Orders, were founded by St Bruno
in 1084 at the monastery of the
Grand Chartreuse, near Grenoble,
south-eastern France. The monks
kept the Rule of St Benedict and it
was they who first produced the
famous green Chartreuse liqueur.
Of only nine Carthusian
monasteries in England, Mount
Grace Priory is the largest and best
preserved. It was founded in 1398
by Thomas de Holland (later Duke
of Surrey who was executed for
treason in 1400) and dedicated to
St Mary and St Nicholas. Having
taken a vow of silence, each monk
lived alone in a tiny cell with his
own private garden. At Mount
Grace there were over twenty
individual cells. After the
Dissolution of 1539 part of the
priory was made into a private
house and one of the cells has now
been restored. The remains are
owned by the National Trust, but
are in the guardianship of English
Heritage.

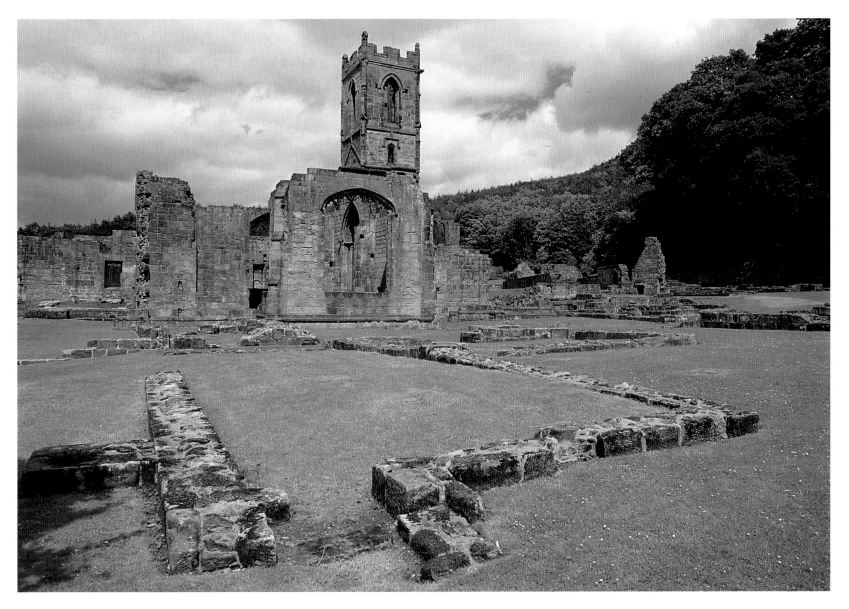

THIMBLEBY FORD
NEAR OSMOTHERLY

The Cod Beck, which enters the Swale near Asenby, is fed by three reservoirs: the upper and lower Oak Dale Reservoirs, on the edge of Thimbleby Moor; and the Cod Beck Reservoir, on Osmotherly Moor. Just beyond the southern arm of Osmotherly, near the late-Georgian Thimbleby Hall, the waters of the beck flow over a small, stepped waterfall and across a tree-lined ford. About a mile to the south, at the foot of the moorland escarpment, is the hamlet of Thimbleby, recorded in the Domesday Survey of 1086 as 'Timbelbi'. Its single, main street forms part of the western boundary of the National Park: those houses to the east lying within the park and those to the west without. The large village of Osmotherly, high above the Vale of Mowbray, was formerly a chartered market town, and by the market cross of 1874 is an old stone table, once used by John Wesley as a pulpit. The Lyke Wake Walk starts a mile or so north of the village.

DANBY HEAD
DANBY DALE

Winter in the North York Moors is often harsh, with heavy falls of snow creating enormous problems for the farmers, whose sheep are often left out on the open moors to forage for themselves. At the mouth, or 'end', of Danby Dale, on the north side of the Esk, lies the small village of Danby, known locally as Danby End. To the east of the village, at Danby Lodge, surrounded by 13 acres of grounds, is the Moors Centre containing a wealth of information about the National Park. The house was formerly a seventeenth-century hunting lodge. Situated in lonely isolation some two miles south-west of the village, in the heart of Danby Dale, is the parish church of St Hilda. Buried in the churchyard is John Christopher Atkinson (1814–1900), the Danby vicar who wrote the minor classic *Forty Years in a Moorland Parish*.

WESTERDALE
from Westerdale Head

From its source high up on Westerdale Moor – where numerous trickling streams unite at the Esklets – the River Esk flows north down Westerdale to Castleton, before heading east to enter the sea at Whitby. The village of Westerdale lies among rich farmland in the heart of the Westerdale valley, and once boasted two inns, a grammar school, two blacksmiths and a wheelwright. Overlooking the village is Christ Church, rebuilt in Gothic style in 1838 and restored in 1875. Beside the river is the former hunting lodge of Westerdale Hall, built in the 1840s by the Duncombes. The Victorian building, with its stepped gables and embattled tower, is now a Youth Hostel. The Duncombe coronet can be seen on the medieval packhorse bridge, which was restored in 1874. The distinctive peak on the horizon in the photograph is Roseberry Topping.

SWALEDALE SHEEP
DANBY HIGH MOOR

Although cattle, pigs and poultry are kept on the lower slopes and floors of the dales, sheep-breeding is the main occupation of the farmers in the North York Moors. Reared for both meat and wool, the most common sheep is the Swaledale, one of the hardiest of breeds, easily recognizable by its black face, white muzzle and speckled grey legs. Both sexes are horned and have long, loose fleeces of coarse, white wool, which helps to protect them against the often hostile climate. They spend as much of the year as possible on the high heather moorland, foraging for themselves in remote areas where many other breeds would not survive. 'Bields', or windbreaks of stone, however, have been built to provide much-needed shelter. It is estimated that as many as 10 per cent of moorland sheep are killed annually on unfenced moorland roads by careless drivers.

DANBY HIGH MOOR

The expansive upland area around Danby High Moor, some 1,400 feet above sea level, is a main watershed, with streams draining north, into Esk Dale, and south, into Rosedale and Farndale. To the north, radiating like the spokes of a giant wheel, are a series of descending ridges, or 'riggs' – Castleton Rigg, Danby Rigg and Glaisdale Rigg. Separating each of the riggs are a number of deep valleys – Westerdale, Danby Dale, Great Fryup Dale and Glaisdale. Over three thousand years ago all of these riggs were occupied by prehistoric people, and evidence of their barrows, burial mounds and rectangular enclosures can be easily found. For example, on Danby Rigg alone – in addition to a 5-foot-high standing stone which is all that remains of a Bronze Age circle some 42 feet in diameter – it has been estimated that there are over 800 small cairns.

LITTLE FRYUP DALE
from Danby Rigg

The two Fryup Dales (Little Fryup and Great Fryup) run parallel to each other, south-west from Esk Dale, to meet at Fairy Cross Plain. The name Fryup is thought to be derived from Friga, an Old English personal name, and 'up' or 'hop', meaning a valley. Each dale contains a stream, named appropriately Little Fryup Beck and Great Fryup Beck, both of which are tributaries of the Esk. There is no village in Fryup, for the cottages and farms that make up the community are scattered throughout both dales. High on the end of Danby Rigg, overlooking the mouth of Little Fryup Dale are the remains of Danby Castle, built by the Latimers in the fourteenth century. Part of the castle buildings have been converted into a farm. Less than half-a-mile north of the castle is Duck Bridge, a narrow, single-arched packhorse bridge spanning the River Esk, thought to date from about 1386.

ARNECLIFF WOOD
GLAISDALE

The numerous paved causeways, or 'trods', found in the region of Glaisdale testify to the fact that the village was once a busy trading centre in the valley of the River Esk. The sandstone slabs have been worn by centuries of use and, when some were turned recently, they were also found to be worn, providing proof that they had been in service for a very long time. The largest stones in the woods of Arncliff (spelt locally Arncliffe) are about 3 feet wide and 6 inches thick. Close by is a large stone, known as the Kid Stone, on which bundles of fire wood (or 'kids') were placed before being loaded onto the packhorse. Since the thirteenth century ironstone has been worked in the valley of Glaisdale, and between 1866 and 1876 the sprawling hillside village housed a large mining community. Today few traces remain of its brief industrial role.

RIVER ESK
EGTON BRIDGE

The River Esk rises on Westerdale Moor, near Esklets, and meanders for some 24 miles through the heart of the North York Moors to empty into the North Sea at the fishing port of Whitby. It is one of the few salmon rivers along the east coast of England, and on their summer-to-autumn run the fish may be seen leaping the weirs at Sleights and Egton Bridge. Much of Esk Dale is thickly wooded, particularly at Crunkly Gill, near Lealholm, and the 3-mile stretch between Glaisdale, Egton Bridge and Grosmont. During heavy flooding in 1930 the stone bridge at Egton Bridge was washed away, and was later replaced with one of iron. The scenic Esk Valley Railway, from Whitby to Middlesbrough, halts at most of the villages in Esk Dale, and at Grosmont is joined by the private North Yorkshire Moors Railway.

BEGGAR'S BRIDGE GLAISDALE

Spanning the River Esk by a high, single arch, Beggar's Bridge stands near the railway station, just east of Glaisdale and on the road to Egton Bridge. It was reputedly constructed for Thomas Ferris, a mariner and shipowner of Hull who lived in the neighbourhood as a youth. It is said he used to ford the Esk by stepping-stones to visit his girlfriend. One day, after he had fallen in and nearly drowned, he vowed that if he made his fortune he would erect a bridge on the spot. Built of stone in 1619, the bridge was designed to carry packhorse traffic, and the low walls lean outwards to allow room for the bulky packs. Today the bridge is open only to pedestrians, and all vehicles have to use the iron bridge which stands beside it.

FALLING FOSS LITTLE BECK VALLEY

Rising on Sneaton High Moor, the May Beck flows south down the May Beck Valley to plunge over the 50-foot precipice of Falling Foss into the wooded ravine of the Little Beck. Just above the waterfall is Midge Hall, a small cottage, built by Sir James Wilson as a home for his gamekeeper. Now derelict, it was once a museum and had an outdoor toilet which emptied over the fall. The Hermitage, about three quarters of a mile downstream, is reputed to have been hollowed out of the sandstone rock by a man called Jeffrey, who also carved two small seats on the top. The inscription above the door 'G. C. 1790' refers to George Chubb, a schoolmaster from the nearby village of Littlebeck. Along the Little Beck Valley there is abundant evidence of abandoned alum and jet workings. There are pleasant woodland trails from Falling Foss along the valleys of both the Little and May Becks.

THOMASON FOSS
BECK HOLE

The tiny hamlet of Beck Hole, with its pub-cum-shop-cum-cafe, lies near the confluence of the Eller and West Becks, and at the foot of the notorious 1,500-yard-long Beck Hole incline. A woodland path leads from the village up the steep northern bank of the Eller Beck to Thomason Foss, a small but attractive waterfall. In the middle of the nineteenth century Beck Hole was a thriving mining community, with two blast furnaces and over thirty stone cottages. All, except the present half dozen or so houses, have disappeared. Algernon Newton, who became a member of the Royal Academy in 1943, purchased the Lord Nelson Inn and converted part of the building into a studio. He was the father of Robert Newton, the film actor, and painted the sign which now hangs outside the Birch Hall Inn.

GOATHLAND STATION
GOATHLAND

Goathland lies on the route of the North Yorkshire Moors Railway. The original line ran up an incline between Beck Hole and Goathland, which was so steep that coaches had to be hauled up by rope. To avoid the notorious incline, the line was re-routed and a new station opened at Goathland in 1865. The high moorland village, just over two miles south of Grosmont, dates from at least the twelfth century. The name is thought to be derived from either 'God-land', after the home of a group of early Christians, or 'Goda-land', after the personal name of a Danish settler. The village is widespread, scattered around a large green – almost a common – on which sheep graze freely. A path beside the hotel, opposite the Victorian church, leads down to the deep, wooded valley of the West Beck, where the 70-foot-high Mallyan Spout waterfall cascades down a moss-covered cliff into the boulder-strewn stream.

Pickering
and the Southern Moors

HAMBLETON HILLS ESCARPMENT

from Whitestone Cliff

Stretching roughly from Hambleton End, above Thimbleby Moor, in the north, to Sutton Bank in the south, the Hambleton Hills lie at the western edge of the North York Moors, overlooking the Vale of York. Running along the crest of the hills is the Hambleton Road, part of an ancient highway linking Scotland with the south of England. It has been used since prehistoric times, and it may have been on this road that William the Conqueror, with a small escort, was caught in a sudden snowstorm and separated from the main body of his army. The road came into its own during the eighteenth and nineteenth centuries, when it was used by Scottish drovers bringing cattle to markets at York and Malton. The advantage of the route was that it avoided the time-consuming and costly turnpikes. Droving declined with the coming of the railways, and by the beginning of the twentieth century the need to move animals long distances on foot had ceased.

Hundreds of thousands of years ago, in the great Ice Age of the Pleistocene period, much of Britain and northern Europe was covered by vast glaciers. These immensely thick sheets of ice – ebbing and flowing like waves, albeit slowly and imperceptibly – drastically re-shaped the surface features of the underlying rock. As the ice advanced it carried with it a mass of debris, including stones, pebbles and boulder clay, which were deposited in morains, banks and barriers. Between these deposits temporary lakes were sometimes formed: the most notable (in north-east Yorkshire) being in Upper Eskdale and the Vale of Pickering. During interglacial periods, however, the region sometime enjoyed a warm, sub-tropical climate. In 1821, while quarrying in Kirk Dale, near Kirkbymoorside, a cave was discovered containing the bones and teeth of animals like the elephant, lion, spotted hyena, woolly rhinoceros, European bison, giant deer and mammoth.

As the last of the great ice-sheets retreated north more than 10,000 years ago, vegetation began to clothe the bare and almost lifeless landscape. By about 6,000 BC, when Britain had almost become an island, North Yorkshire was covered by a dense forest of birch and pine, mixed with oak, alder and hazel. The first people to exploit the natural resources of the forest were Mesolithic groups of hunters, fishermen and food-gatherers. Their impact on the environment, however, was minimal. They were followed by the first farmers, a Neolithic (New Stone Age) people who came from mainland Europe in about 3,000 BC. Although evidence of their settlements in the North York Moors is sparse, Neolithic long barrows can be seen at East Ayton near Scarborough, at Scamridge south-east of the Dalby Forest, and on the Hambleton Hills near Kepwick.

The process of clearing the forest and tilling the soil was accelerated by the arrival of the people of the Bronze Age in about 1,500 BC. They built most of the stone circles, cairns and round barrows (tumuli) found scattered throughout the moorland. None have survived complete, for over the years many of the stones have been used in the construction of gate-posts and walls. Principal remains of stone circles can be found at: Danby Rigg; Blakey Topping, east of the Hole of Horcum; Flat Howe and High Bride Stones, both on Sleights Moor near Grosmont; Standingstones Rigg, 6 miles north-west of Scarborough; and Bride Stones, a 40-foot-diameter circle on Nab Ridge, 9 miles north of Helmsley.

The belief that these prehistoric monuments were inhabited by fairies and goblins was prevalent in the countryside until well into the nineteenth century. Reputed to appear at night to plague or assist the farmers, according to their mood, these supernatural beings are remembered in the names of many of the sites..

Obtrusch, who favoured a tumulus on Rudland Moor above Farndale, made the life of one of the farmers so unbearable that in desperation he decided to leave. Loading all his possessions onto a cart, the farmer set off down the dale relieved that he was rid of the troublesome creature once and for all. On the way, however, a neighbour happened to comment: 'Ah see thoo's flittin!' Before the farmer could reply, a cheeky hobgoblin voice echoed back from inside a churn. 'Aye, we's flittin!' With a sigh, the farmer, resigned to defeat, turned his horse and returned to his farm.

Prehistoric boundary dykes, or earthworks, dating from about 1,000 BC, can also be found in the region, most notably in the southern moors to the east of Newton Dale. Although there are numerous dykes on the Hambleton Hills between Sutton Bank and Kepwick, the most spectacular and best-preserved are at Scamridge. Records confirm that many of these ancient dykes continued to be used in medieval times, particularly by monastic houses for delineating the limits of their lands. For example, in 1142 the Hesketh Dyke, on the hills north-east of Boltby, formed the northern boundary of the original Byland estate at Old Byland, before the abbey was moved to Stocking and finally Byland. Even today, some of these dykes continue to be used to mark boundaries.

By 500 BC, when the people of the Iron Age first began to appear in Britain, the climate was much colder and wetter than today. Iron Age settlements in the North York Moors tended to be sited on the well-drained, sheltered slopes of the hills. Two of their settlements can be found on Kildale Moor, south of Guisborough, and Great Ayton Moor nearby. Among the Iron Age hill-forts in the region are: Eston Nab, east of Middlesbrough; Roulston Scar, near Sutton Bank; Live Moor, above Swainby; and possibly Oliver's Mount, overlooking Scarborough. It was from these, and similar strategically placed forts around the western and southern moors, that the Iron Age tribesmen, called Brigantes, made their final stand against the advancing might of Rome.

BECK ISLE COTTAGE THORNTON-LE-DALE

Thornton-le-Dale, often called Thornton Dale, lies just within the boundary of the National Park, about 2 miles east of Pickering. The suffix '-ton' indicates an Anglo-Saxon settlement. Mentioned in the Domesday Book as 'Torentune', it was not until the early nineteenth century that 'Dale' appeared in the name. One of the many attractive features of Thornton-le-Dale is the sparkling trout-frequented Thornton Beck, which runs in stone channels alongside the streets, past picture-postcard cottages and underneath low stone footbridges. On the small village green, in the shadow of an old chestnut tree, there is a worn market cross and wooden stocks. The parish church of All Saints, at the eastern end of the village, dates from the fourteenth century, with a chancel rebuilt in 1866. The Almshouses and Grammar School were both founded by Lady Elizabeth Lumley in 1656. The thatched cottage in the photograph – Beck Isle Cottage – dates from the sixteenth century and stands, set back, on the north side of the main road, between the almshouses and the church.

PICKERING CASTLE

There is a tradition that the settlement of Pickering was established in 270 BC by the British King Peredurus, who gave it the name 'pike-a-ring', after his lost ring had been recovered from the stomach of a locally caught pike. The market town of 'Pichering', situated at the southern edge of the Moors, was held by William the Conqueror himself at the time of Domesday. He hunted in Blansby Park, part of the Royal Forest of Pickering, and built a castle on the hill high above the town. The original castle consisted of a great moated mound, or motte, surrounded by ditches and protected by timber palisading. Most of the present stone fortress dates from between 1180 and 1326 and now belongs to English Heritage. The parish church of St Peter and St Paul in Pickering contains several unique fifteenth-century wall paintings, depicting Biblical, historical and legendary scenes.

THROXENBY MERE THROXENBY

On the outskirts of Scarborough, to the west of Throxenby, is a small lake formed towards the end of the Ice Age. In pre-glacial times the River Derwent flowed into the North Sea at the eastern end of the Vale of Pickering. When its original course was blocked by ice-borne debris, it carved a new route south through Forge Valley and west across the Vale of Pickering, eventually entering the sea through the Ouse and Humber. Glacial meltwaters deepened the Forge Valley, while flooding the low lying vale to the south. In the nineteenth century an artificial channel, known as the Sea Cut, was dug to divert most of the water from the Derwent into the sea at Scarborough. This had a twofold effect in the Vale: it reduced the danger of flooding and also improved the land for agricultural use. The woods in the photograph are the eastern continuation of Raincliffe Woods which lead into the deeply wooded Forge Valley, now a nature reserve.

NORTH YORKSHIRE MOORS RAILWAY NEWTON DALE

Designed by George Stephenson, the 24-mile Pickering-to-Whitby line was originally a horse-drawn carriageway. Officially opened on 26 May 1836, its route took it north from Pickering, through Newton Dale to Goathland, Grosmont and, eventually, Whitby. In 1845 George Hudson, 'the railway king', financed the conversion of the line to take trains pulled by steam locomotives. Although locomotives were in operation on the southern part of the line, it was two years before the first locomotive reached Whitby. The line was taken over by the North Eastern Railway Company in 1861 and four years later the section between Goathland and Beck Hole was re-routed to avoid the impossibly steep incline. From then on, for the first time, steam power was used throughout the entire route. Although the line was closed in 1965, the section between Grosmont and Pickering was re-opened by the North York Moors Historical Railway Trust in 1973.

HOLE OF HORCUM LEVISHAM MOOR

On the western side of the main road from Whitby to Pickering, near the Saltergate, is the spectacular natural amphitheatre of the Hole of Horcum – an enormous hollow which was excavated many thousands of years ago by Ice Age meltwaters and the erosive action of springs. It was once believed that the mysterious 300-foot-deep depression was the work of the Devil or a giant called Wade. According to one tradition, the Devil scooped out a handful of earth and cast it across the moors. The hollow he created became known as the 'Devil's Punchbowl', or the Hole of Horcum, while the handful of earth he threw became the 876-foot-high Blakey Topping, about a mile to the east. It is also said that the marks left by the fingers of the Devil can still be traced on the slopes of the Hole. At the foot of the hill to the north is the remote Saltergate Inn, once the haunt of smugglers.

ST HILDA'S CHURCH
ELLERBURN

Less than a mile north of Thornton-le-Dale, in the secluded, tree-flanked valley of Thornton Beck, lies Ellerburn, a small hamlet noted for its ancient church. Although it has been restored more than once, the church of St Hilda possesses abundant examples of work from the Saxon and Norman periods. It has a chancel, nave, porch and virtually no tower, while the interior contains an eighteenth-century pulpit which was once used by a former caretaker for hatching his hen's eggs. There are two interesting cross-heads: an Anglo-Danish wheel-head cross of the tenth century and a crucifix cross of the eleventh century. In the churchyard is the Dobson Monument – a red granite obelisk with a grey stone finial, erected in 1879 in memory of Robert Dobson who died 8 September 1825. The lychgate leading to the church was constructed in 1904. In the not too distant past, Ellerburn was a small industrial area, with paper mills to the north and a quarry to the south.

LOW BRIDESTONES
GRIME MOOR

There are several Bridestones throughout the Moors: on Nab Ridge, Bilsdale; near Silpho; and on Black Brow, Sleights Moor. The rocks in the photograph are on Grime Moor at the north-western edge of Dalby Forest. They can be reached from Stain Dale by a circular walk which climbs high above Dove Dale. The Low Bridestones stand to the east of Bridestones Griff, while the High Bridestones stand to the west. These outcrops of Jurassic rock, each made up of varying layers of hard and softer sandstones, were fashioned by the elements into their present surreal shapes. They are in the care of the National Trust. The origin of the name Bridestones is uncertain, but they may be connected with ancient fertility rites. According to one tradition, the name arose when a newly married couple from Lockton were caught in a thick mist on their way to Scarborough and were forced to seek shelter among the rocks.

WADE'S CAUSEWAY
WHEELDALE MOOR

On Wheeldale Moor, about 3 miles south-west of Goathland, are the remains of Wade's Causeway – a Roman road which stretches north-east across the North York Moors from the Vale of Pickering to an undiscovered point on the coast, possibly near Kettleness or Whitby. The road has been called Wade's Causey, Wade's Wife's Causey and sometimes The Auld Wife's Trod. It is known locally as Wade's Causeway, after a Saxon chieftain called Wade, or Wadde. According to legend, Wade was a giant who lived at Mulgrave Castle with his equally huge wife, Bell. It is said that he built the causeway to make it easier for Bell to take their cattle to market across the marshy moorland. In reality the road was constructed around 1,900 years ago by the Romans as part of a military network which extended from the legionary fortress of Derventio at Malton. Wade's Causeway passes through Cawthorne Roman Camps, some 4 miles north of Pickering. The stretch in the photograph is 16 feet wide and around 1¼ miles long.

EARLY WARNING STATION
FYLINGDALES MOOR

A celebrated moorland landmark, the hugh, white spherical domes of the Ballistic Missile Early Warning Station at RAF Fylingdales have been variously described as giant 'ping-pong balls', 'golf balls' or more correctly 'radomes'. They were constructed on Ministry of Defence land between 1961 and 1962 to give advance warning of a nuclear attack, commencing full operation in January 1964. Each one, weighing over 100 tons, is 140 feet in diameter and 154 feet high on its black rectangular plinth. The globes were in fact designed to protect the three large radars, each one 84 feet across, from the elements. Over the years the station has been used mainly for its secondary role of space surveillance, tracking some 2,000 satellites a week. In August 1989, on a more prominent hill-top site, work began on the construction of a 120-foot-high truncated pyramid to replace the familiar 'golf balls'. Close by, on Lilla Howe, almost 1,000 feet above sea level, is the seventh-century Lilla Cross, believed to be the oldest Christian memorial in the north of England. It was moved to its present site in 1952 by the Royal Engineers to avoid destruction from gunfire on artillery ranges.

SOUTH FRONT
CASTLE HOWARD

Henderskelfe Castle, dating from the end of the eleventh century, was destroyed by fire in 1693 only ten years after being rebuilt. Five years later Charles Howard, 3rd Earl of Carlisle, having quarrelled with his first choice of architect, turned to the dramatist and former soldier, John Vanbrugh, for designs for a new house to be built on the castle site. Up until that moment, Vanbrugh's architectural experience was nil. Nevertheless, working closely with the architect, Nicholas Hawksmoor, he produced one of Yorkshire's greatest houses: a Baroque masterpiece, described by Horace Walpole as 'a palace, a town, a fortified city'. Work began in 1700 and progressed slowly for over fifty years, during which time much of the landscape architecture was completed. The house was finished by Sir Thomas Robinson, the 4th Earl's brother-in-law, who was responsible for building the Palladian west wing, completed in 1759. The dome was destroyed by fire in 1940 and rebuilt in the early 1960s.

TEMPLE OF FOUR WINDS
CASTLE HOWARD

The old village street of Henderskelfe, recorded as 'Hildreschelf' in the Domesday Book, now follows the line of the terraced walk to the Temple of Four Winds, designed by Vanbrugh in Palladian style. He died in 1726, before it was completed. The Temple's white and gold interior is embellished with scagliola and plasterwork by Francesco Vassali. The South Lake, constructed in 1724, was formalized by William Nesfield in the 1860s, who also added the Cascade, Temple Hole and the Waterfall, which links the South Lake with New River. Hawksmoor designed the magnificent Mausoleum, built between 1731 and 1742, which Walpole thought 'would tempt one to be buried alive'. The landscaped grounds of Castle Howard, containing numerous architectural gems, is as richly rewarding as the house itself, which contains a wealth of treasures. It is situated near Malton, 15 miles north-east of York, in the Howardian Hills.

KIRKHAM PRIORY

On the east bank of the River Derwent, some 5 miles south-west of Malton, are the remains of the Augustinian priory at Kirkham. It was founded in about 1122 by Walter l'Espec, Lord of Helmsley, and is reputed to have been built to commemorate his son, Walter, who was thrown from a horse and killed. L'Espec also founded the Cistercian abbey at Rievaulx, and it may be because of his support for the newly arrived monks from Clairvaux that the Augustinian canons at Kirkham almost joined the new Order. Although negotiations took place, the transfer of those who wished to stay in the Augustinian order to a new house at Linton was never carried out. Kirkham Priory remained Augustinian until its dissolution in 1539. The late thirteenth-century gatehouse is decorated with carved sculptures and the heraldic shields of its founder and patrons. The property is in the care of English Heritage.

VALE OF PICKERING NEAR NUNNINGTON

Towards the end of the Ice Age, the Vale of Pickering was occupied by a vast lake, thought to cover an area of not less than 160 square miles. It stretched from near Ampleforth, where the Vale of York glacier trapped the water to the west, to Wykeham, south of Pickering, where a similar obstruction blocked its exit to the east. Although the lake disappeared thousands of years ago, it left behind some of the richest farmland in the north of England. The photograph is taken from near Keepers Cottage, west of Nunnington village, looking across the flat, fertile valley of the River Rye towards the southern edge of the North York Moors. Nunnington Hall, nearby, is a stone manor house set in attractive gardens on the banks of the Rye. It dates from 1552, but was badly damaged during the Civil War and was restored at the end of the seventeenth century. It is owned by the National Trust and contains the Carlisle Collection of Miniature Rooms.

HUTTON-LE-HOLE

Until the Dissolution Hutton-le-Hole was owned by the Benedictine monks of St Mary's Abbey at York. Recorded simply as 'Hotun' in the Domesday Book, the present village lies on a slope at the southern edge of the North York Moors, 2 miles north of Kirkbymoorside. With its limestone houses, shops and inns scattered at random around a long, undulating village green, the village is a popular tourist centre. The oldest buildings date from the seventeenth century, when many of the Quaker families wove woollen cloth in their own homes. The house on the left of the photograph is Ford Cottage, and was once the home and workshop of the village carpenter. On the extreme right is Primrose Hill Farm, built in the traditional 'longhouse' style to shelter people and animals under the one roof. The Hutton Beck rushes through the middle of the white-railed green, where grazing sheep keep the grass short.

WAYMARKER
SPAUNTON MOOR

Standing by an ancient ridgeway close to the present Blakey Road, nearly 2 miles north of Hutton-le-Hole, is a good example of a stone waymarker, probably erected in 1712. On the west side is carved a hand, the initials 'R.B.' and 'R.E.' and 'Road to Kirkbymoorside'. On the north side is 'Road to Gisborough' with a hand pointing to the sky. On the east side is 'Road to Pickrin or Malton', with a hand pointing south. These stones are variously called 'waymarkers', 'guide stones' and those with roughly carved hands, 'handstones'. The oldest routes across the moors were the ridgeways, such as Blakey Rigg and Rudland Rigg, keeping to the high, firm ground above the dales. On the slopes they were often worn into narrow, deep hollow-ways or hollow tracks. The Kirkbymoorside waymarker stands beside a hollow-way, some 6 feet deep and 8 feet wide.

ST MARY'S CHURCH
LASTINGHAM

St Cedd, a Lindisfarne monk, founded a monastery at Lastingham in AD 654. Ten years later, before it was finished, Cedd died of plague and was, eventually, buried in the church. The Celtic monastery was probably destroyed by the Danes in about 870. Rebuilding, however, did not commence until 1078, when William the Conqueror gave Abbot Stephen of Whitby permission to settle at Lastingham with a colony of monks. Stephen built a Norman crypt over the site of St Cedd's shrine, and above it began to erect a great abbey church. It was never completed, for in 1086 Stephen moved to York where he founded St Olave's and, later, St Mary's Abbey. The present church at Lastingham, completed in 1228, incorporates part of Stephen's building, including the apsidal crypt, which is preserved almost unaltered since it was first built over 900 years ago. The south aisle was widened and the bell tower erected in the fourteenth century.

ROSEDALE
from Rosedale Head

The River Seven rises on Danby High Moor, near Young Ralph Cross, to flow south-east down the 7-mile-long valley of Rosedale, eventually joining the Rye in the Vale of Pickering. Nestling in the heart of the dale is Rosedale Abbey, a small village which takes its name from the Cistercian nunnery founded sometime before 1158 by William de Rosedale. The priory (never an abbey) of St Mary and St Lawrence was severely damaged by Scottish raiders after the battle of Byland in 1322 and dissolved in 1535. Much of the building survived until 1850, when large quantities of stone were used in the construction of houses during the Rosedale ironstone boom. Apart from the remains of a tower and a few walls, all that is left of the priory has been incorporated into the parish church of 1839. On Cropton Bank, near the mouth of Rosedale, are the earthwork remains of a Norman motte-and-bailey castle.

NEAR LOW MILL
FARNDALE

Every spring, between March and May, the banks of the River Dove are covered with mile after mile of wild yellow daffodils, known locally as Lenten Lilies, for they bloom around Easter. The plants and the bulbs, which thrive in damp woodlands, are protected by law and in 1953 2,000 acres of Farndale were designated as a local nature reserve. Farndale is thought to mean Fern Valley, but may derive its name from *fearna*, the Gaelic word for alder. The upland village of Gillamoor stands at the southern end of Farndale, some 500 feet above sea level, with a 'surprise view' overlooking the remote valley. St Aidan's parish church was built in 1802 by James Smith, a local stonemason, who, according to a wall plaque, was 'a sound workman and completed it with his own hands'. The church was restored in 1880 and as a precaution against high winds has no north or east windows.

LOW MILL
FARNDALE

Farndale is a long, narrow valley with steep sides, enfolded by the moorland heights of Rudland Rigg, Farndale Moor and Blakey Rigg. Unlike most of the moorland dales, Farndale is not named after the river which flows through it, nor is there a village of that name. Instead, isolated farmhouses and cottages are scattered throughout the dale, which also contains three small but distinct hamlets: Church Houses, Low Mill and Lowna. Jet, coal, ironstone and gravel have all been worked in Farndale or on the moors above it. In the 1930s Hull Corporation planned to flood the upper part of the valley to create a reservoir. The idea was revived in 1967 by the Yorkshire Ouse and Hull River Authority, but after a 10,930-strong petition had been sent to Parliament the plan was postponed.

ALL SAINTS' CHURCH
KIRKBYMOORSIDE

Situated almost midway between
Pickering and Helmsley at the
southern extremity of the North
York Moors, the ancient town of
Kirkbymoorside contains a market
square, a steep, cobble-lined main
street and numerous coaching inns,
the earliest – the Black Swan –
dated 11 October 1632. The name
means the 'village with a church on
the edge of the moors', but was
recorded in 1282 as 'Kirkeby
Moresheved', or Kirkby
Moorshead, which refers to its
elevated position above the Vale of
Pickering. The church of All Saints
dates from the twelfth century and
was built on the site of an earlier
church. It was considerably altered
over the centuries. The west tower
was rebuilt in 1802, and restoration
by George Gilbert Scott between
1873 and 1875 included the
rebuilding of the chancel. On the
hillside above the church are the
remains of a castle probably built
by the Stuteville family who owned
the town in Norman times.

SMOUT HOUSE
BRANSDALE

Sheltered beneath the high, wild
moorland of Bilsdale East Moor,
Bransdale Moor and Rudland
Rigg, Bransdale is one of the
remotest valleys in the North York
Moors. Smout House lies on the
north-eastern slopes of the dale,
between Toad Hole and Yoad
House, just over a mile south-east
of the tiny hamlet of Cockayne. The
two-storeyed farmhouse was built
in the early nineteenth century on a
centralized plan, with a central
front door and rooms to either side.
During the eighteenth century, the
yeoman farmers began to copy the
houses of the gentry, moving away
from the traditional, linear,
longhouse plan to squat,
symmetrical, box-like buildings.
Longhouses were difficult to
convert to a centralized layout, but
some attempts were made by
inserting doorways between
forehouse and parlour or by
rebuilding. There are a number of
examples of adapted and converted
longhouses in Bransdale. Nearly
2,000 acres of farmland in the
valley is now owned by the
National Trust.

ST GREGORY'S MINSTER KIRKDALE

Rising on Bransdale Moor, the Hodge Beck flows south-eastward through Bransdale and the deep, wooded gorge of Kirk Dale, before entering a subterranean channel near Hold Cauldron. After heavy rain or floods the surplus water is carried along the surface bed to eventually join the re-emerging underground spring below Welburn Hall. During the summer, the ford at Kirkdale is often dry. Close by, in an old quarry, is the entrance to a cave in which the bones of prehistoric animals were discovered in 1821. On the opposite side of the beck is the lonely and secluded church of St Gregory's Minster, dating from Anglo-Saxon times. The Saxon sundial above the south doorway records that in about 1060: 'Orm, son of Gamal, bought St Gregory's Minster when it was all broken down and fallen and he let it be made anew from the ground . . . in the days of Edward the King, and of Tostig the Earl.' The small tower was added in 1827 and the chancel rebuilt in 1881.

EAST MOORS

Heather moorland is the natural habitat of the red grouse (*Lagopus lagopus scoticus*) – a truly wild game bird, about the size of a small chicken – which spends the entire year within its breeding area. It was once regarded as an exclusively British species, but is now considered a sub-species of the willow grouse (*Lagopus lagopus*). The adult male has a dark reddish-brown plumage, with bright red wattles over the eyes and white feathered legs. Often, it has the startling habit of springing straight up, almost from beneath the feet of walkers, in a chattering explosion of whirring wings. The male's distinctive challenge to rivals seems to say 'Go-back! go-back! go-back!' There are a number of grouse butts on East Moors. On the eastern side of the Helmsley-to-Cockayne road, which runs across East Moors, is the little church of St Mary Magdalene, designed by Temple Moor in 1882. It lies in a clearing, surrounded by conifers, a short distance north of Cowhouse Bank Farm.

EAST MINES
ROSEDALE

In 1851 the inhabitants of Rosedale totalled 558. Twenty years later the figure had more than quintupled to 2,839. This dramatic increase in population was due entirely to the discovery of a rich vein of high quality iron-ore in the area of Hollins Farm, about a mile south of Rosedale Abbey. Although ore had been mined in the region from at least the Middle Ages, it had never been on such a large or intensive scale. Between 1856, when the Hollins or West Mines were opened, and 1885, when they were finally closed, some three million tons of iron-ore were removed from the hillsides. The arrival of the railway in 1861 and the opening of more mines escalated production. The closure of the East Mines in 1926 marked the end of ironstone mining in Rosedale. By 1971 the population had declined to 225. The remains of calcining kilns can be seen in the photograph.

ALL SAINTS' CHURCH
HELMSLEY

Straddling the southern border of the National Park, the popular market town of Helmsley lies in a sheltered corner of upper Rye Dale on the north bank of the River Rye. Major roads from York, Thirsk, Stokesley and Pickering converge upon its spacious market square, in the centre of which is a canopied monument to the 2nd Lord Feversham who died in 1867. The nearby market cross was moved around 300 years ago from its original site in the churchyard. Tucked away behind the houses, shops and hotels of the square is the parish church of All Saints, built in the thirteenth-century style between 1866 and 1869. Although it has often been rebuilt, parts of the structure date from Norman times. The Domesday Book mentions that there was a church at 'Elmeslac', or Helmsley, in 1086. North of the church is Canons' Garth, a restored Tudor house built by the canons of Kirkham, who once owned the church.

HELMSLEY CASTLE

After the Norman Conquest, King William I granted Helmsley to his half-brother, Robert de Mortain. His lands were confiscated in 1088 and shortly afterwards the manor passed to William l'Espec. Although there was almost certainly an earlier fortress on the rocky site, the present castle was built by Robert de Roos, Lord of Helmsley from 1186 to 1227. Standing immediately to the west of the town, the keep and curtain walls date from the de Roos time, while the barbican, guarding the main entrance, was built in the mid-thirteenth century. The domestic buildings, including the Great Hall, were altered towards the end of the sixteenth century by Edward Manners, 3rd Earl of Rutland. The castle was damaged during the Civil War and on the death of the Duke of Buckingham the estate was sold to Sir Charles Duncombe, a wealthy London Banker. It now belongs to English Heritage.

RIEVAULX ABBEY

In 1131 Walter l'Espec, the Norman Lord of Helmsley, granted land beside the River Rye to a colony of thirteen Cistercian monks from Clairvaux. Rievaulx Abbey was founded on the site and within twenty years the community was said to number 140 monks and 500 lay brothers. For the last two years of his life, l'Espec himself became a monk at the abbey and was buried in the church. Rievaulx was the first Cistercian house in the north of England and soon became one of the great mother churches of the Order in Britain. Although its main source of wealth was from sheep-farming, the brothers were also involved in mining, fishing, agriculture and tanning. The abbey was dissolved in 1538 and its last abbot, Sedburgh, was hanged at Tyburn for suspected involvement in the rebellion known as the Pilgrimage of Grace. The name Rievaulx comes from a Franco-Norman word meaning 'valley of the Rye'. The remains of the abbey are owned by English Heritage.

NEWBURGH PRIORY
NEAR COXWOLD

Just outside the southernmost extremity of the National Park are the sparse remains of the Augustinian priory of Newburgh, founded in 1145 by Roger de Mowbray and dedicated to St Mary. After its dissolution in 1538, Henry VIII granted the priory to his chaplain, Anthony Belasyse, whose descendant Lord Fauconberg married Mary, the daughter of Oliver Cromwell. There is a persistent tradition that Mary secretly obtained the headless body of her father, after it had been hung on Tyburn, and buried it in a vault at Newburgh. The slight remains of the priory have been incorporated into the present, essentially eighteenth-century mansion. Less than a mile north-west of the priory is the small, compact village of Coxwold, the home of the novelist Laurence Sterne (1713–68), who wrote *Tristram Shandy*. He became vicar of Coxwold in 1760 and lived at Shandy Hall, now a Sterne museum. Although he was originally buried in London, his remains were removed to Coxwold in 1969.

SILVER HILL
NEAR SNECK YATE

The derelict buildings of Silver Hill Farm, near Sneck Yate Bank, lie on the Boltby-to-Hawnby road, high on the Hambleton Hill limestone escarpment, 994 feet above sea level. The Hambleton Drove Road and the Cleveland Way pass close by. On the summit of Boltby Scar, 1,090 feet above sea level, are the earthwork remains of an Iron Age promontory fort. Within the nearly 3-acre semicircular area there are also three Bronze Age barrows, or burial mounds. Silver Hill tumulus is 60 feet in diameter and 6 feet high. Hesketh Dyke, a prehistoric boundary dyke, runs east from the scarp edge to Moors Ings Bank and was used in medieval times by the monks of Old Byland Abbey. Below Sneck Yate Bank ('yate' meaning gate) is the ancient village of Boltby, with a Victorian chapel designed by William Burn and a little stone bridge.

BYLAND ABBEY
NEAR WASS

In 1143, after several moves, a colony of Savigniac monks, originally from Furness Abbey, was granted land by Roger de Mowbray to the west of the River Rye, near Old Byland. Twelve years earlier, the Cistercian Abbey of Rievaulx had been founded on the opposite bank of the river. It was not long before the close proximity of the two houses became totally unacceptable. The bells of one could be heard by those of the other at all hours of the day and night, and eventually the newcomers were persuaded to move. In 1147 Mowbray gave them a new site at Stocking, near Oldstead. That same year, the Savigniac Order was absorbed into the Cistercian Order and the monks at Stocking became Cistercian. Although they remained at Stocking for thirty years, the site became too small for the growing community and in 1177 they made the final move to Byland. The remains of this once great abbey are in the care of English Heritage.

VALE OF YORK
from Roulston Scar

Roulston Scar lies in the south-western corner of the National Park, a short walk south along the Cleveland Way from the Sutton Bank Information Centre. On the steep southern escarpment of Roulston Scar, above the village of Kilburn, a white horse has been carved in the limestone. It is 314 feet long and 229 feet high and was cut out of the turf in 1857 by a Kilburn schoolmaster, with the help of the villagers. The horse can be seen up to 70 miles away and is a useful landmark for gliders using the airstrip on top of the Scar. Kilburn is also noted for the furniture workshops of Robert Thompson (1876–1955), whose trade-mark of a carved mouse can be found in hundreds of churches, including Westminster Abbey and York Minster. From Sutton Bank there are walks and nature trails along the top of the escarpment and down the steep slopes to Lake Gormire.

York and the Vale of York

YORK MINSTER

from the City Walls

York Minster, the largest medieval cathedral in Britain, is the fourth to stand on the site. The first church was built of wood by Edwin, King of Northumbria, who was converted to Christianity by his wife, Ethelburga (whom he married in AD 625), and her chaplain, Paulinus. Erected on the site of the former Roman Principia, it was soon replaced by a cathedral of stone. The Saxon building was damaged by fire in 741, by the Danes in 867 and by the Normans in 1069. In 1070 Archbishop Thomas of Bayeux began building the Norman Minster. It was damaged, together with St Mary's Abbey and many other churches, when an accidental fire devastated the city in 1137. The present Minster was built between 1220 and 1480, when the 234-foot central tower was completed. On 9 July 1984 the south transept was badly damaged by fire. The undercroft contains a museum depicting the entire Minster's history. The Deanery Gardens are in the foreground of the photograph.

Some thirty years after the Roman invasion of Britain in AD 43, the legions had reached the thickly wooded Vale of York and were advancing north into the Moors and Dales. In AD 71 Petrillius Cerialis built a fortress on the banks of the river Ouse, near its confluence with the Foss. Known as Eboracum, Roman York became the administrative capital of the province of Britannia Inferior and the northern military headquarters of the Imperial army. It was at Eboracum, after the death of his father Emperor Constantius Chlorus in AD 306, that Constantine the Great was proclaimed Emperor.

After the withdrawal of the Roman legions at the beginning of the fifth century, there was a period of confusion and disorder. The invading Angles, who had probably reached York by about the year 500, found the city in ruins, and made it the capital of their kingdom of Deira, to the east. Edwin, the Anglo-Saxon King of Northumbria, was baptised at York, then called Eoforwic, on Easter Eve 627. An enthusiastic convert to Christianity, he made Paulinus the first Bishop of York and built a wooden cathedral on the site of the present Minster. Alcuin, a brilliant scholar and native of York, who became the head of the York cathedral school and a famous luminary at the court of Charlemagne, commemorated the city in his poem on 'The Bishops, Saints and Kings of York' composed in about 792. He describes it as a walled stronghold, an inland port and a prosperous merchant town, 'watered by the fish-rich Ouse / Which flows past flowery plains on every side'.

In November 866 a Danish army, sailing up the Humber and the Ouse, occupied York and, in the following year, placed a puppet king, the Anglo-Saxon Egbert, on the throne of Northumbria. Despite repeated attempts by the Anglo-Saxons to recapture the city, Jorvik, as it was known, became the capital of the Danish kingdom of York. Excavations in the city, particularly at Coppergate, have revealed that the Vikings were not merely 'pirates' but were also sophisticated traders and craftsmen. York was the centre of a thriving economic community, and at the Jorvik Viking Centre is a reconstruction of part of the Anglo-Danish settlement at Jorvik, with houses, workshops, full-scale human figures, sounds, smoke and even smells.

Evidence that many of the Danes settled down peaceably with their Anglo-Saxon neighbours and became farmers, can be found in the names of numerous places scattered all over the Vale of York, the eastern dales and the southern moors. Those, for example, with the suffix -*by* (meaning village) are fairly positive indicators of a former Danish settlement: Easby, Melmerby, Thorlby, Slingsby, Whitby, and the many variations of Kirkby ('a village with a church'). A large number of the suburbs around York have names with the suffix -*thorpe* (an old Danish word meaning a secondary settlement, or hamlet).

At the beginning of the tenth century north-west Yorkshire was invaded by the Norsemen, who came to the western Dales by way of Cumbria and Lancashire. Originating from Norway, these new settlers had colonized the Scottish Islands, the Isle of Man and eastern Ireland before crossing the Irish Sea into northern England. Even today many of the settlements in the central and western Dales have Norse rather than Danish or Anglo-Saxon names. *Thwaite* ('a woodland clearing') is the name of a village in Swaledale and also occurs as a suffix in place names, like Yockenthwaite.

On 25 September 1066, at Stamford Bridge, 8 miles east of York, Harold, the last Saxon King of England, defeated the Danish army under Harald Hardrada, King of Norway. Three days later, the Normans invaded, landing at Pevensey on the south coast, and by the end of the year William, Duke of Normandy, had been crowned King of England.

Several towns, including York, defiantly objected to Norman rule. Yet, when William arrived at the gates of the city in 1068, he was allowed to enter without resistance. He immediately ordered the construction of a castle on the site of what is now known as Baile Hill and stationed a garrison in the city. Early the following year, the townspeople rebelled. As soon as the king appeared with his army, however, the insurgence quickly collapsed. In order to strengthen his control of the city, William erected a second castle on the site of the present Clifford's Tower. A further revolt, on 19 September 1069, supported by the Danish king, Swein Estrithson, succeeded, and the inhabitants captured both castles and killed almost every Norman in the city.

William's revenge was cruel and remorseless. During the winter of 1069–70 his army devastated Northumbria, burning houses, pillaging food-stores and slaughtering the inhabitants. In what came to be known as the Harrying of the North, vast areas of the countryside were laid to waste. York, consumed by flames, never rebelled against Norman rule again.

STONEGATE
YORK

Following the line of the Roman Via Praetoria, the ancient street of Stonegate leads from St Helen's Square (the site of the main, Praetorian Gate) to York Minster (the site of the Principia, or military headquarters). The present street lies literally on top of the Roman roadway. The name is thought to be of Scandinavian origin, meaning 'the stone-paved street'. During medieval times limestone, quarried at Tadcaster, was taken up Stonegate to build the Minster. The street was closed to traffic in January 1971 and contains a fascinating mixture of medieval and Georgian architecture. Outside No. 33 is a little, red, chained devil – a reminder that the shop was once a printers, for 'printer's devils' were the small boys who used to fetch and carry type. Mulberry Hall, dating from the fifteenth century, was formerly a merchant's house. The oldest and narrowest street in York is the Shambles, and is the only street in York mentioned in the Domesday survey of 1086.

CLIFFORD'S TOWER
YORK

After the Norman invasion of 1066, William the Conqueror ordered the construction of a motte-and-bailey castle at Baile Hill on the west bank of the River Ouse. A few years later a second castle was built on the opposite bank of the river, where Clifford's Tower now stands. In order to create a moat around the second fortification, the Foss – a tributary of the Ouse – was dammed, which flooded 120 acres of farming land and formed a lake known as the King's Fishpool. During the reign of Henry III (1216–1272) a new stone castle was built to replace the earlier wooden structure. The curtain walls, with towers and two large gatehouses, enclosed an area of some 3 acres. The keep, or Clifford's Tower, is of an unusual quatrefoil design and stands on a mound about 40 feet high. Apart from a substantial stretch of curtain wall, the 33-foot-high tower is all that remains of the royal castle.

GUILDHALL
YORK

The Guildhall, St Helen's Square, stands on the east bank of the River Ouse near Lendal Bridge. It is reached through an archway to the side of the Mansion House and is a reconstruction of the original hall, built by Robert Couper in the middle of the fifteenth century. It was destroyed by German incendiary bombs in 1942, rebuilt in 1958 and re-opened on 21 June 1960 by Queen Elizabeth the Queen Mother. The Mansion House, built in 1725–7, is the official residence of the Lord Mayor of York during his year of office. St Helen's Square was formerly the churchyard of St Helen's Church, which according to tradition, is built on the site of a Roman temple to Diana. Across the city, in St George's churchyard, is the grave of the legendary highwayman Dick Turpin – known then as John Palmer – who was hanged at York in 1739.

ST MARY'S ABBEY
YORK

The ruins of St Mary's Abbey
stand to the west of the Minster,
just outside the city walls and in the
gardens of the Yorkshire Museum.
Founded for Benedictine monks in
1088 by William Rufus, the abbey
was originally founded before 1086
by Count Alan of Brittany, Earl of
Richmond, on a smaller site at
nearby Marygate and dedicated to
St Olave. The community came to
York, from Whitby Abbey by way
of Lastingham. In 1132 a reformist
group of thirteen monks left St
Mary's to found Fountains Abbey.
St Mary's grew to be one of the
largest and wealthiest Benedictine
houses in the north. It was
dissolved in 1539, and during the
eighteenth century the stone was
used for many buildings in the city,
including the reconstruction of St
Olave's Church. The remains
include parts of the church, the
abbot's lodging (incorporated in
King's Manor), the Hospitium and
the gatehouse in Marygate. Every
four years the ruins provide a
backdrop to the York Mystery
Plays.

MULTANGULAR TOWER
YORK

Situated in the spacious gardens of
the Yorkshire Museum, the
Multangular Tower was built in
about AD 300 and stood at the west
corner of the walled Roman fortress
of Eboracum. Although it is about
28 feet high, it is Roman only to a
height of some 17 feet – the rest was
added in the thirteenth century.
The tower has ten sides and was
given the name 'Multangular',
meaning 'many-angled', in 1683 by
Martin Lister, a York physician
and amateur historian who was the
first to realize its Roman origin.
Attached to the tower is a
substantial length of fortress wall,
containing the remains of a smaller
tower. Further buildings of interest
in the Museum grounds include:
the ruins of St Mary's Abbey; the
remains of St Leonard's Hospital,
dating from the thirteenth century;
and the Observatory, built in 1832
and containing material relating to
the York astronomer, John
Goodricke, who discovered the star
Algol.

DEVIL'S ARROWS
BOROUGHBRIDGE

In a field at the western edge of the former coaching town of Boroughbridge, beside the busy A1 main road, are a line of three millstone grit pillars, each standing about 20 feet high. Local legend says that the devil took a strong dislike to the nearby settlement of Aldborough and determined to destroy it. Having warned the inhabitants of Boroughbridge to keep out of the way, he climbed to the top of How Hill (3 miles south-west of Ripon) and threw four huge stones towards Aldborough. Known as the Devil's Arrows, each one fell short of its target. The fourth stone has long since been removed: one half of it is reputed to lie in the grounds of Aldborough Manor; the other half was used in the construction of a bridge over the little River Tut. The monoliths date from the Bronze Age and are thought to have been transported from a quarry near Knaresborough, 7 miles south-west.

SAINT MARY'S CHURCH
THIRSK

Considered to be the best example of Perpendicular architecture in Yorkshire, St Mary's Church dates from the fifteenth century. The west tower, with its stepped buttresses, is 80 feet high. In the grounds of nearby Thirsk Hall, dating from about 1720, is the stump of the ancient market cross. Lying in the centre of the fertile Vale of Mowbray, the busy market town is divided by the Cod Beck, a tributary of the Swale: to the east is Old Thirsk, centred around its village green, formerly the market place; while to the west is New Thirsk, established during the eighteenth-century coaching era when the town became a major staging point on the route from London to the north-east. James Herriot, the world-renowned author and vet, based 'Darrowby' on the bustling market town, with its wide, cobbled square, old coaching inns, restaurants and shops.

RIPON CATHEDRAL

Ripon Cathedral, sometimes called Ripon Minster, stands on the site of a Saxon church founded by St Wilfrid in AD 672. Although the church was destroyed by the Danes in 860, the crypt survived – and still survives, despite the building of two later churches, including the present cathedral. It is the earliest crypt to be found in an English cathedral and is reached by a 45-foot-long passage, leading underneath the central tower from an entrance near the nave choir stalls. The Minster, which was refounded as a collegiate church in 1604, became the cathedral church of the newly formed diocese of Ripon (which covers most of the Dales and also Leeds) in 1836. Dedicated to St Peter and St Wilfrid, the medieval cathedral – built of local millstone grit – stands on a hill-top site to the east of the ancient market town, overlooking the valley of the River Ure.

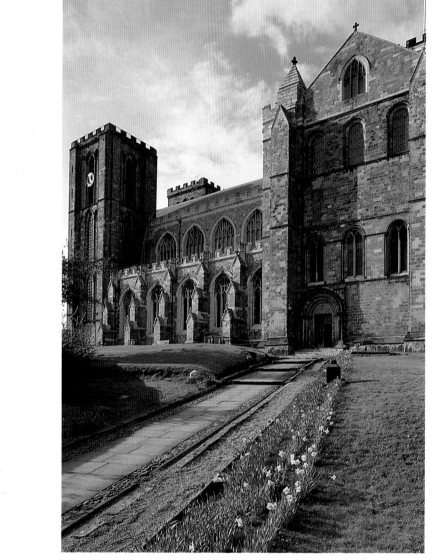

DRUID'S TEMPLE
NEAR ILTON

Evidence of Prehistoric man's presence in the North Yorkshire landscape thousands of years ago includes standing stones, cairns, and even stone circles. But, despite appearances, the Druid's Temple near Ilton is not of ancient origin. It is in fact a folly and was erected in about 1820 by William Danby of nearby Swinton Hall, who based its design on that of Stonehenge. It is, however, lozenge-shaped – over 100 feet long and 50 feet wide – and consists of various stone arrangements called: The Two Outer Guards; The Two Inner Guards; The Sacrificial Altar; The Four Columns; The Phallus; The Wardens or Priests; The Master or Hierophant; The Two Guards of Solar Temple; The Solar Temple; and The Tomb. The massive stone lintel over the entrance is over 10 feet long. Hidden in a conifer plantation, between the reservoirs of Leighton and Ilton, the temple is some 4 miles south-west of Masham. It can be reached by a short woodland walk.

The Yorkshire Dales

WEST BURTON FALLS

In the narrow, limestone gorge below West Burton there is a series of attractive waterfalls, fed by Walden Beck. Rising on the north-eastern flanks of Buckden Pike, over 2,300 feet above sea level, the waters of the beck flow north for almost 5 miles – through Waldendale – to West Burton, beyond which they tumble over the falls, and under an old packhorse bridge, to enter the Bishopdale Beck just before joining the Ure. The ancient village of West Burton, Wensleydale, mentioned in the Domesday survey of 1086, lies on the east side of Bishopdale, just over a mile south of Aysgarth. Bordered by grey-brown stone houses and cottages, the wide, sloping green was formerly used for fairs. However, instead of the usual preaching cross, it contains a stepped, stone spire, erected in 1820 and crowned by a weather-vane. Above and to the east of West Burton is Penhill, reaching 1,726 feet above sea level.

During the Carboniferous period, some 280 to 330 million years ago, the Yorkshire Dales were covered by a shallow tropical sea, the floor of which was formed of even older Silurian, Ordovician and Pre-Cambrian grits, slates and shales. Slowly, over vast periods of time, thick layers of sedimentary deposits were laid down on this ancient bedrock in a monumental geological sandwich; the lowest stratum being Great Scar limestone, or Mountain limestone. Formed under immense pressures from the powdered shells of primitive sea organisms, this fine-grained, grey-white rock is a characteristic feature of much of the central and south-western Dales. It is particularly striking at Malham Cove and Gordale Scar, in Airedale, and at Kilnsey Crag, in Wharfedale.

On top of the Great Scar limestone, further sediments were deposited in thinner, alternating layers of shales, sandstones and limestones. This particular sequence of rock strata is known as the Yoredale Series, from their greatest concentration in the dale of the River Ure, formerly Yore, in Wensleydale. Since the shales and sandstones erode faster than the limestones, the typical Yoredale landscape has been weathered into long, horizontal terraces, stepped by steep little cliffs, known as scars. Although prominent in Wensleydale, the effect can also be seen, for example, on the north-eastern slopes of Ingleborough, where the Yoredale Series sits conspicuously above the Great Scar limestone. Another characteristic of the Yoredale landscape is the abundance of waterfalls, among the most impressive of which are Hardraw Force and the Aysgarth Falls in Wensleydale.

Above the Yoredale Series is a sequence of thick, coarse-grained sandstones, separated by wide bands of shales. Known as millstone grit, the rock was used by millers during the Middle Ages for grindstones. Much of the surface of the eastern Dales is composed of this gritstone, but the rock also caps the summits of western peaks like Ingleborough and Whernside. In places – most notably at Brimham Rocks, near Pately Bridge in Nidderdale – outcrops of the rock have been sculpted by erosion into fantastic and spectacular shapes. Between the millstone grit and the Yoredale Series there are often seams of coal, many of which were extensively worked in the eighteenth and nineteenth centuries.

During the formation of these various rocks, periodic movements of the earth's crust remorselessly reshaped and remodelled the surface of northern Britain. Land masses rose and subsided, repeatedly. Overwhelmed by the strain of untold pressures, the assorted layers of sedimentary rock folded, heaved and buckled as if made of plasticine. In areas like Crummack Dale and Ribblesdale, the ancient Ordovician and Silurian rocks were pushed to the surface through the younger Carboniferous rocks. While the even older Pre-Cambrian green and blue slates were exposed in the vicinity of Ingleton, and can be clearly seen, for example, below the limestone strata at Thornton Force.

Further geological unrest caused great cracks, or faults, to appear in the sedimentary rocks. Strata, once continuous, fractured, slipped and dropped vertically, sometimes by thousands of feet, to create the great cliff faces of Malham Cove, Gordale Scar and Giggleswick Scar. There are two main landslips in the region: the Craven Faults in the southern Dales, running roughly east to west from Pately Bridge towards Kirkby Lonsdale; and the Dent Fault in the western Dales, running roughly north to south along the Rawthey Valley, across lower Garsdale, and down Barbondale. In addition, volcanic activity to the west forced molten rock, containing lead ore and other minerals, upwards into weak points in the rock structure.

Over the ages, climatic conditions have also played a major role in the moulding and shaping of the landscape. Some rocks, being softer than others, are less resistant to weathering. Limestone, for example, is water-soluble and, in time, the erosive action of running water has not only been responsible for the formation of many features above ground, but has also created a vast network of potholes, passages and caverns underground.

Periodically, the land was covered by vast sheets of ice, sometimes lasting for millions of years. Glacial action gouged out pre-existing valleys, transported small rocks and gigantic boulders sometimes hundreds of miles, and deposited vast quantities of clay, stones and gravel. Finally, about 12,000 years ago, the last great ice sheet withdrew to reveal the bare but familiar bones of the present Yorkshire Dales.

Designated in 1954, the Yorkshire Dales National Park covers an area of 680 square miles. Although most of the Park is in North Yorkshire, the north-western corner lies in Cumbria. Traditionally, however, the Yorkshire Dales embrace a much larger area than that enclosed by the Park boundaries. In broad terms the Dales are bounded in the east by the Vale of York, in the west by the River Lune, in the north by the River Tees, and in the south by the River Wharfe.

GORDALE SCAR NEAR MALHAM

Gordale Scar, just over a mile north-east of Malham, is a deep, narrowing gorge – guarded by precipitous limestone cliffs – which terminates in a dark and eerie amphitheatre. Here, the Gordale Beck pours through a natural hole in the rock wall to create a series of small waterfalls. The glazed, ripple-like rock supporting the falls is 'tufa', a porous reconstituted stone formed by deposits of limestone. It was originally thought that the gorge was once a gigantic underground cavern, the roof of which has collapsed. But an alternative theory suggests that it was carved by the erosive action of glacial meltwater. Thomas Gray visited the gorge in 1769 and, venturing to within 12 feet of the fall, wrote: 'there are loose stones that hang in the air, and threaten visibly some idle spectator with instant destruction . . . I stay'd there (not without shuddering) a full quarter of an hour, and thought my trouble richly paid, for the impression will last for Life.'

Richmond
and the Northern Dales

MIDDLEHAM CASTLE
WENSLEYDALE

The first castle at Middleham, built to guard the entrances of Coverdale and Wensleydale, was of the Norman motte-and-bailey type. Its ruins lie in Sunskew Park, some 500 yards south-west of the present castle, and date from about 1086, when Alan, Earl of Richmond, granted the manor of Middleham to his younger brother Ribald. It is thought that the present castle, with its massive, rectangular keep – one of the largest in England – was begun in the middle of the twelfth century. It became one of the strongholds of the Nevilles, Earls of Warwick, but was forfeited to the Crown in 1471. For a number of years, it was the principal residence of Richard, Duke of Gloucester, later Richard III. Having become uninhabited towards the end of the fifteenth century, some of its stone was used as building material. Today the remains are in the care of English Heritage. The market town, which occupies the outer bailey, is famous for breeding and training racehorses.

Determined, once and for all, to remove any further threat to Norman rule in England from the insurgent people of the north, William the Conqueror devastated and depopulated vast areas of the Yorkshire countryside. Those who managed to flee from the systematic slaughter, returned to find their farms sacked and their houses burned. To escape starvation, many were forced to leave, or sell themselves and their families into slavery; others remained to simply perish. The extent of the decimation can be gleaned from the Yorkshire section of the Domesday Book, compiled in 1086, seventeen years after the Harrying of the North. Out of some 1,900 manors or villages mentioned, around 850 were seemingly uninhabited, while a further 300 were simply referred to as waste, *Wasta est*.

The manors recorded in the Domesday survey lie solely in the eastern and southern Dales, penetrating into the uplands only as far as Stainforth in Ribblesdale, Starbotton in Wharfedale, Askrigg in Wensleydale and Reeth in Swaledale. Beyond these outlying settlements, the land was officially designated forest – vast tracts of countryside, not necessarily wooded – which became the hunting preserve of the new Norman nobility, with horrendous penalties for anyone caught poaching the 'protected' game. The Norman lords of Skipton hunted Littondale and Langstrothdale Chase; the lords of Middleham exploited Wensleydale Forest and Bishopdale Chase; while Swaledale and Arkengarthdale Forest were the exclusive domain of the lords of Richmond.

In order to control the upland passes through the eastern Dales, as well as the lowland routes between Scotland and England, the Normans erected castles at strategic locations, first of wood and later of stone. Barnard Castle, a few miles beyond the north-eastern boundary of the National Park, guarded Teesdale and the southern approach to the Vales of Mowbray and York; while Skipton Castle, in the extreme south, protected the Aire Gap – an important pass across the Pennines, which rises no higher than 400 feet above sea level. Middleham Castle, with its massive twelfth-century keep, defended Coverdale and the entrance to Wensleydale; while the cliff-top fortress at Richmond commanded the mouth of Swaledale. Further castles were built at Bowes near Barnard Castle, Ravensworth near Richmond, Ripley near Harrogate, and Hornby near Bedale. Bolton Castle in Wensleydale was constructed from about 1379 by the first Lord Scrope for defensive purposes, but with particular emphasis on domestic comfort.

To take advantage of the protection afforded by these great fortresses – as well as to cater for the needs of their garrisons – towns grew up outside their walls: some evolving from small, pre-existing settlements. The rise in population resulted in an increase in trade and, inevitably, these early Norman castle-towns soon became important market centres for the produce and livestock of the surrounding countryside. The towns which were granted the right to hold weekly markets and annual fairs, grew and prospered even further, most notably Richmond, Middleham and Skipton. Those who benefited most, however, were the Norman lords, as they received a significant and steady income from the tolls levied on all goods sold.

Although the Norman aristocracy, who built and lived in the castles, were responsible for the original development of many of these market towns, the most powerful and lasting influence on the economy and landscape of the Dales came from another foreign over-lordship – the medieval monasteries.

Almost as soon as they had established themselves in their fortresses, the feudal lords began to encourage the building of religious houses, inviting monks over from Europe, mainly France, to found abbeys and priories of the various monastic orders. Apart from the Benedictines, among the first to settle in the Dales were the Cistercian monks of Fountains Abbey, founded in 1132 by Thurstan, Archbishop of York. They were followed in 1145 by the Cistercians of Fors, near Askrigg, who moved to Jervaulx in 1156. Premonstratensian canons settled at Easby, near Richmond, in 1151 and, three years later, the community of Augustinian canons at Embsay, near Skipton, moved to Bolton in Wharfedale. Other foundations followed, including two small nunneries in Swaledale (a Benedictine priory at Marrick in about 1158 and a Cistercian priory at Ellerton). The Premonstratensian abbey at Swainby, 6 miles south-west of Northallerton, founded in about 1187, moved to Coverham, near Middleham, in 1202.

For some four hundred years, from foundation to dissolution, the medieval monasteries increasingly dominated the economy of the Dales. Having been granted most of the wild, upland country – land which was of little use to the Norman lords – they became the major landowners in the region. With great expertise, particularly in sheep-rearing and iron-making, they set about transforming the uncultivated wilderness into a flourishing land of plenty. Draining swamps and clearing huge areas of scrubland, it was the monasteries who laid the foundations of much that is so characteristic of the Dales landscape of today.

SWALEDALE
from near Gunnerside

The headwaters of the River Swale rise on the peaty, moorland heights of Birkdale Common, Angram Common and Stonesdale Moor. In actuality, the Swale begins at the place where the Great Sleddale Beck meets the Birkdale Beck. From its endlessly trickling origins, the river plunges eastward to Keld – descending rapidly down the wooded gorge between East Stonesdale and Kisdon – before meandering south to Muker. In the 20 miles between Muker and Richmond the river – flowing swiftly eastward over its stony bed – passes through some of the most characteristic scenery of the Dales: lush green water-meadows, field-barns and dry-stone walls, all surrounded by steep, grassy hillsides. Beyond Richmond, the 'Gateway to Swaledale', the Swale winds south-eastward to enter the Ure in the Vale of York, 2 miles east of Boroughbridge. The photograph is taken from just east of Gunnerside looking west up Swaledale towards Great Shunner Fell.

RICHMOND

from 'Maison Dieu'

Situated at the entrance to Swaledale, the ancient market town of Richmond stands on a prominent hill-top site to the north of the River Swale. The cobbled market place, almost semicircular in shape, was formerly the outer bailey of the castle. In the middle stands Holy Trinity Church, dating from Norman times, with shops built into its walls. Pevsner calls it 'the queerest ecclesiastical building one can imagine'. It is now the Regimental Museum of the Green Howards. The ancient market cross was removed in 1771 and replaced with an obelisk. Many of the narrow alleys and streets in Richmond are known as 'wynds'. Legend tells of a drummer boy who was lowered into an underground passage beneath the town. The sound of his beating drum was followed above ground until it ceased half a mile from Easby Abbey. The boy was never seen again.

RICHMOND CASTLE

In 1068 William the Conqueror granted lands in Yorkshire to Alan the Red of Brittany, later Earl of Richmond, as a reward for his services. Three years later Alan began building a castle and residence on a cliff overlooking the River Swale. The town which grew up around the Norman fortress became known as Richmond: derived from the French *Riche-mont*, meaning 'strong hill'. The rectangular keep, which unusually stands right over the original gatehouse, was added by Earl Conan the Little in about 1150 and completed during the reign of Henry II. It is over 100 feet high with immensely thick walls and, for greater security, was reached by an entrance on the first floor. In addition to the Great Tower, Richmond castle has a second keep: the eleventh-century Scolland's Hall, named after Earl Alan's steward. The remains of the castle are now in the care of English Heritage.

EASBY ABBEY
NEAR RICHMOND

Less than a mile south-east of Richmond, on the north bank of the River Swale, Easby Abbey was founded in about 1155 for Premonstratensian canons by Roald, Constable of Richmond Castle, and dedicated to St Agatha. It was one of forty abbeys and three nunneries founded in England under the Order, which also included Coverham, 3 miles south of Leyburn. Little is known about the early history of Easby Abbey. During the Middle Ages it was damaged by Scottish raiders and in 1346 by English troops who were billeted there during a military campaign. Unlike most medieval abbeys which were built on a similar plan, Easby is unusually laid out on a skew because of the lie of the land. The abbey was demolished after the Dissolution and its remains are in the care of English Heritage. Nearby, the small thirteenth-century parish church contains some medieval frescoes.

NEAR IVELET

Some of the finest hay meadows in the Dales can be found in upper Swaledale, between Gunnerside and Muker. They are at their best in late June or early July in an average year. Most of the fields contain a large stone barn to store the hay and house the cattle during the winter months. Names for the barns vary depending on the area: in Swaledale they are called 'field-houses' or 'cow-houses'; in Wharfedale and Craven they are called 'laithes'. Since the mid-1950s the use of artificial fertilizers has almost doubled the yields of hay. But in the process the rich variety of wild flowers and grasses which flourished in the old, naturally manured meadows has greatly diminished. A few meadows, however, are still farmed the traditional way, and some – like Yelland's Meadow at Muker owned by the Yorkshire Wildlife Trust Ltd – have become nature reserves. Ivelet is located in upper Swaledale, just over a mile west of Gunnerside.

LANGTHWAITE ARKENGARTHDALE

The most northerly dale in the National Park, Arkengarthdale is a tributary valley of Swaledale and was once the hunting preserve of the Norman Lords of Richmond. Its river, the Arkle Beck, rises on the heights of Arkengarthdale Moor to flow south-east down the valley – past Whaw, Eskeleth, Langthwaite, Arkle Town and Booze – to the market town of Reeth, above the River Swale. Its name and the names of its settlements are of Norse origin: Arkengarthdale meaning 'the valley of Arkil's garth' or field. The surrounding fellsides are scarred by the decaying remains of lead-mining, an industry which flourished in the area until the end of the nineteenth century. Coal was transported by road down the valley from Tan Hill colliery to fuel the smelting furnaces around Langthwaite – the main settlement in the dale. The village was featured in the BBC television series *All Creatures Great and Small*, its small bridge appearing in the original title sequence.

OLD GANG MINES SWALEDALE

Lead ore has been extracted from the Dales since prehistoric times. After the Norman Conquest, it was in great demand for the roofing of castles and churches, and many of the abbeys increased their income by working iron as well as lead. The main lead-mining area in the northern Dales was in Swaledale and Arkengarthdale. But it was not until the seventeenth century that intensive mining began. By the beginning of the nineteenth century, Britain was the world's largest exporter of lead. Because of cheaper imports from abroad, however, the industry fell into a decline: and by the end of the century mining in the Dales had virtually ceased. In the triangle of land between Swaledale and Arkengarthdale the landscape is scarred with the remnants of the lead-mining industry, including spoil heaps, smelting hearths, peat stores and chimneys. The ruins of the Old Gang mining complex can be reached by walking to the head of Hard Level Gill from Surrender Bridge, on the Feetham-to-Arkengarthdale road.

RIVER SWALE
UPPER SWALEDALE

From Keld the River Swale – tumbling over a series of dramatic falls – rushes south-east down a wooded limestone gorge, before sweeping south in a long, sinuous 'S' bend to Muker. Standing below Buzzard Scar, on the wooded slopes north of the confluence of the Swale and Swinner Gill, are the ruins of the eighteenth-century Crackpot Hall – originally a shooting-lodge, later a farmhouse, and abandoned because of lead-mining subsidence. The name 'Crackpot' is derived from the old Norse meaning 'pothole of the crows'. It is passed by the long-distance Coast-to-Coast Footpath. To the left of the valley in the photograph (taken from near Crackpot Hall) are the steep slopes of Black Hill, rising to 1,683 feet; while to the right the escarpment rises 1,637 feet to the grassy summit of Kisdon, once known as 'Kisdon Island'. In the distance is Muker Common, enclosed by dry-stone walls in the early nineteenth century.

MUKER COMMON
NEAR THWAITE

Kisdon, an isolated hill over 1,630 feet high, dominates the head of Swaledale and is flanked by a trio of villages: Keld in the north, Muker in the south-east and Thwaite in the south-west. The largest of the three villages is Muker, with its grey stone cottages, late sixteenth-century church (much altered in later centuries), inn, Literary Institute, and shops (including Swaledale Woollens which sells local hand-knitted garments). 'Muker' (pronounced 'Mooker') and 'Thwaite' are derived from old Norse words, meaning 'a small, cultivated field' and 'a woodland clearing', respectively. Thwaite was the birthplace of the Kearton brothers, Richard (1862–1928) and Cherry (1871–1940), pioneers of natural-history photography. The stone lintel of their home is carved with birds and animals. They are also commemorated at Muker, where they went to school. To the south, across the Straw Beck, a tributary of the Swale, lies Muker Common, rising to 2,215 feet at Lovely Seat.

WAIN WATH FORCE NEAR KELD

Situated below the limestone cliff of
Cotterby Scar, a short distance
upstream of Park Bridge and less
than a mile north-west of Keld,
Wain Wath Force is one of a series
of waterfalls on the upper reaches
of the River Swale. Three miles
north, on the West Stones Dale
Road from Keld, is the lonely Tan
Hill Inn, the highest inn in
England, 1,732 feet above sea level.
It lies exactly on the northern
boundary of the National Park and
provides a welcome stopping-place
for walkers on the Pennine Way. At
the crossing-point of routes from
Keld, Arkengarthdale and Brough,
the eighteenth-century inn was
used, among others, by Scottish
drovers on their journey south.
Within the vicinity, the windswept
moors are pitted with the derelict
remains of old mine workings.
Some of the coal extracted from the
rocky wilderness was employed
locally for smelting the lead ore.

THE BUTTER TUBS NEAR THWAITE

The Butter Tubs – an unusual
group of deep holes in the limestone
– lie, some 2 miles south-west of
Thwaite, close to and on either side
of the 1,726-foot-high mountain
pass road linking Wensleydale and
Swaledale. They were supposedly
called 'Butter Tubs' because the
farmers from Muker, returning
from Hawes market, lowered their
unsold butter in baskets deep inside
the chasms to keep it cool –
retrieving it the following week on
the way back to the market. Some
say, however, that the limestone
columns which separate the holes
resemble old-fashioned butter tubs.
These long, fluted columns have
been formed over the centuries by
water (combined with the cracking
action of frost) dissolving parts of
the limestone strata. The holes are
between 50 and 90 feet in depth
and should be approached with
care. It is reported that one female
visitor asked a local shepherd how
deep they were: 'Very deep,
ma'am,' he replied. 'Some's
bottomless, and some's even deeper
than that.'

HARDRAW FORCE

England's highest waterfall above ground, Hardraw Force, lies at the head of a limestone gorge to the north of the village of Hardraw, near Hawes in upper Wensleydale. Often spelt 'Hardrow', the falls are reached through the Green Dragon Inn and along a path which leads to the entrance of the gorge, where there are the remains of a bandstand and overgrown terraced seats: a reminder that brass band concerts were held in the natural amphitheatre during the late nineteenth century. These have been periodically revived in recent years. The force plunges unbroken some 96 feet and it is possible – albeit with heart-in-mouth – to walk behind the fall in the shelter of the rocky overhang. Above the force, in Shaw Gill Wood, are further waterfalls, which, if less spectacular than the main fall, are far more attractive. Wordsworth and his sister Dorothy visited 'Hardraw Scaur' in December 1799.

COW SIDE
COVERDALE

The 12-mile-long Coverdale is the largest of Wensleydale's tributary valleys. Its entrance is guarded by the ruins of Middleham Castle, and it can also be reached from Wharfedale at the other end by a tortuous road which climbs steeply north-east from Kettlewell to the Iron Age earthworks of Tor Dyke, over 1,650 feet above sea level. From here the road drops down – past Cow Side – over 800 feet into Carlton, the largest village in the dale, close to which is a conical Norman motte. The remains of the Premonstratensian Coverham Abbey – originally founded at Swainby, near Thirsk in about 1187 – lie in private grounds, near the foot of the valley. At the very head of the dale is Hunter's Stone, placed there by the monks to mark the moorland route from Coverham to Kettlewell. The photograph was taken near Woodale, looking across the deep gorge of one of the many gills which flow into Coverdale's River Cover.

HAWES
WENSLEYDALE

At 850 feet above sea level, Hawes is one of the highest market towns in England. It stands at the meeting-point of roads from Richmond, Leyburn, Skipton, Settle, Ingleton, Sedbergh and Kirkby Stephen. Although it was originally part of a Norman hunting forest in Upper Wensleydale, the first recorded mention of the settlement was not until 1307. As time passed it gradually expanded, particularly as a result of the packhorse trade, and in 1700 it was granted its first market charter. Growth further increased with the re-routing of the turnpike road in 1795 and the arrival of the railway in 1877. The line was closed in 1964, and the station buildings now house the National Park Information Centre and the Upper Dales Folk Museum. With its long main street, bisected by narrow lanes and alleys, Hawes remains an important market centre, where thousands of sheep and cattle are auctioned each year.

SEMER WATER
NEAR BAINBRIDGE

Held back by a glacial moraine, Semer Water – $1^1/2$ miles in circumference – is the largest natural lake in Yorkshire. It lies in a deep hollow, some 800 feet above sea level, on the southern side of Wensleydale. According to local legend an ancient city lies drowned beneath its surface. The 2-mile-long River Bain, which issues from the lake, is reputed to be England's shortest river. Near the confluence of the Bain and the Ure, at Brough Hill by Bainbridge, are the earthwork remains of the Roman fortress of Virosidum. A well-preserved stretch of Roman road – which ran for 19 miles between Brough and Ingleton – can be seen on a long spur of Wether Fell, south-west of Brough. The nearby village of Bainbridge, with its broad green, ancient inn, wooden stocks and restored mill, was founded in the mid-twelfth century by Robert, son of Ralph, after he had been granted the wardship of Wensleydale Forest.

HOLY TRINITY CHURCH WENSLEY

On the north bank of the River Ure in Wensleydale, 1½ miles south-west of Leyburn, the village of Wensley stands round a small green at the entrance to Bolton Hall. Its importance as a medieval market centre led to the entire valley being named after it. After the population had been devastated by an outbreak of plague in 1563, the market moved to Leyburn and Askrigg. Its church, however, remains as evidence of Wensley's former prosperity. Considered to be the finest church in the National Park, it dates from 1245 and was built on the site of an earlier Saxon foundation. Further additions and improvements were carried out in the fourteenth and fifteenth centuries, and in 1719 the west tower was rebuilt. The interior contains many reminders of the powerful Scropes of Bolton Castle, who were patrons of the church: notably the seventeenth-century family box pew and a screen which came from the Scrope chantry in Easby Abbey after the Dissolution.

UPPER AYSGARTH FALLS

Aysgarth, in upper Wensleydale, lies on the southern banks of the River Ure, 4 miles downstream from Askrigg. It derives its name from *Eik Skard*, meaning 'an open space marked by oaks'. The church and Youth Hostel lie about half-a-mile east of the main village, not far from where the river is crossed by a narrow, single-arched stone bridge, thought to date from 1539. From Yore Bridge, as it is called, can be seen the spectacular Upper Aysgarth Falls, where the river cascades over three broad limestone steps, or terraces – formed by the erosion of the thin beds of soft shale beneath the limestone blocks, from which sections have broken off and been washed away. The Middle and Lower Falls can be reached by a woodland footpath running alongside the north bank of the river. Opposite the church (mainly rebuilt in 1866) and the Yorkshire Museum of Carriages and Horse-drawn Vehicles (formerly a mill), is the National Park Information Centre, with car park, toilets and shops.

BOLTON CASTLE
CASTLE BOLTON

Bolton Castle, at the eastern extremity of the National Park, occupies a strategic position above Wensleydale, on the south-eastern flank of East Bolton Moor, 4 miles west of Leyburn. The village of Castle Bolton, with its stone cottages bordering the green, is thought to have been laid out at the end of the fourteenth century when the castle was constructed. The church – dwarfed by the soaring walls of the castle – dates from the same period and has, unusually, no structural division between the nave and chancel. Built as a fortified manor by Richard Scrope, Lord Chancellor of England, the castle is four-square: 180 feet long, 130 feet wide, with corner towers nearly 100 feet high. Mary Queen of Scots was held prisoner there from July 1568 to January 1569, before her eventual execution. After the Civil War, the castle was partly dismantled and remained unoccupied, by an order issued in 1647, for some 300 years. It is now open to the public.

JERVAULX ABBEY
NEAR EAST WITTON

In 1145 Acarius Fitz Bardolf, Lord of Ravensworth, founded a religious house at Fors, near Askrigg, for Savignac monks from Byland Abbey. Two years later, the Savignac and Cistercian Orders were united. The abbey, having become Cistercian, moved to a new site in 1156 at Jervaulx – on the banks of the River Ure, between Middleham and Masham. The land was given to them by Conan, son of Alan, Earl of Richmond, and from modest beginnings the abbey became one of the leading abbeys in Yorkshire. Revenue came from iron- and coal-mining as well as sheep-farming. It is reputed, that the monks were responsible for making the first Wensleydale cheese. They also bred horses. The abbey was destroyed in 1537 by Henry VIII and the last abbot hanged at Tyburn for his involvement in the revolt known as The Pilgrimage of Grace. 'Jervaulx' is derived from Yorevale (the vale of the Yore or Ure). The photograph shows the ruins of the chapter house.

Skipton
and the Southern Dales

BOLTON PRIORY
BOLTON ABBEY

The ancient village of Bolton Abbey – owned by the Trustees of the Chatsworth Settlement – lies in Wharfedale, just inside the southern boundary of the National Park, some 4 miles north-west of Ilkley. The nearby monastic ruins, standing on the west bank of the River Wharfe, are those of a priory, and not an abbey. The Augustinian house was originally founded in 1120 at Embsay, 4 miles to the west, near Skipton. Building began on the priory in 1154, when the canons moved to Bolton, and the work was largely completed by 1220. Increased prosperity from mining and wool sales – despite incursions by the Scots in the fourteenth century – led to improvements and additions to the priory. Construction of the great west tower, started in 1520, was halted less than twenty years later by the Dissolution. The nave is now in use as the parish church, dedicated to St Mary and St Cuthbert. Nearby Bolton Hall is the Yorkshire residence of the Duke of Devonshire.

In 1131 Bernard of Clairvaux (1090–1153) sent Abbot William and twelve monks to Yorkshire to found Rievaulx Abbey, the first Cistercian monastery in the north of England. One year later, a reformist group of Benedictine monks left St Mary's Abbey in York to found a monastery in the valley of the River Skell, on land given to them by Thurstan, Archbishop of York. Unable to cope with the appalling hardship, the monks turned to Bernard of Clairvaux and the Cistercian Order for held. In the autumn of 1135 Fountains, as the abbey came to be called, was admitted into the order and, by the middle of the thirteenth century, it had become one of the wealthiest religious houses in England.

It was not only Fountains, and the other local monasteries, which were granted large estates in the Dales: others from further afield, like Furness, Sawley, Bridlington, and Byland, also became major landowners. Between them, Fountains, Furness, Byland and Sawley owned most of the rich limestone country between Ribblesdale and Wharfedale; Rievaulx had extensive rights of pasture in upper Swaledale; Jervaulx owned most of the upper part of Wensleydale north of Askrigg; Coverham and Easby had land in the area of Sedbergh and Garsdale; Bridlington owned much of Swaledale; Bolton owned upper Airedale; and Byland and Fountains shared Nidderdale.

Although they exploited the mineral wealth of the land, it was through sheep-farming on a large scale that the monasteries – especially those of the Cistercian Order – grew and prospered. They built up a lucrative international trade in wool, and from the thirteenth to the sixteenth centuries large quantities of Yorkshire fleeces were exported, via York, to Europe, particularly Florence and Venice.

In addition to clearing hundreds of acres of rough scrubland, draining water-logged valleys and improving the quality of the pastureland, the monasteries established granges on the distant uplands. These outlying farms were connected to their mother houses by an extensive network of packhorse routes, many of which still survive as green tracks, or stone causeways, across the fells. When the site of a proposed grange was found to be occupied, the monasteries either expelled the tenants or gave them the option of staying on as labourers. The management of the granges was delegated to lay brothers, or *conversi*, who were employed by the monks (notably the Cistercians) to undertake much of the routine manual work, both inside and outside the monastery.

Between the thirteenth and fourteenth centuries, an increase in the population of the Dales created a demand for more arable land. As the valley floors and sides were already under cultivation, the medieval peasants were forced to exploit the unploughed pasture-land higher up the hillsides. On slopes, often steep, they gradually created, by ploughing, a stepped series of long terraces, or strip lynchets. Most follow the contours of the hillsides, and may be 100 or even 200 yards long and perhaps 20 yards wide. The Black Death of 1346–8, however, decimated the population, sometimes wiping out whole settlements, and, with the sudden availability of better-quality land lower down the slopes, the strip lynchets became redundant. Although some may be of Anglo-Saxon origin, there are excellent examples of these now-grassed-over medieval terraces in Wensleydale (between Castle Bolton and Carperby), in Wharfedale (between Grassington and Burnsall), in Littondale and in Airedale (around Malham).

Most of the dry-stone walls, so characteristic of the Dales landscape of today, were built between 1760 and 1820, when a series of Enclosure Acts were passed by Parliament. These acts enabled the landowners to enclose much of the old unfenced common land by stone walls, creating neat rectangular fields of 8–12 acres. In most of the fields a two-storeyed, stone barn was built to store hay and house cattle over the winter months. The total number of these barns found scattered throughout the region may well run into thousands, for there are about a hundred alone within a square mile of the village of Muker in Swaledale. This combination of stone walls and field barns is a distinctive feature of the landscape of the Dales and is found nowhere else in Britain.

Despite the dramatic changes brought about during the Industrial Revolution of the nineteenth century, with the coming of the railway and the establishment of mining communities, farming still remains the major activity in the Dales. The colder climate, shorter growing season and thinner soils of the upland areas, however, has meant that farming is essentially pastoral, with sheep predominating over cattle. Sheep have been a vital part of the economy and evolution of the landscape for hundreds of years. It is appropriate, therefore, that the emblem of the Yorkshire Dales National Park is the head of a Swaledale ram.

ST MICHAEL AND ALL ANGELS' CHURCH HUBBERHOLME

Situated between the steep wooded slopes of Langstrothdale in upper Wharfedale, the ancient hamlet of Hubberholme is thought to derive its name from Hubba, a ninth-century Viking chieftain. The squat, grey-stone church, dating from the twelfth century, was originally a forest chapel, and in 1241 it was given to the monks of Coverham Abbey. Inside the church is a rare rood loft and screen, painted red, black and gold, dated 1558. The carved pews, bearing the mouse trademark of Robert Thompson of Kilburn, were installed in 1934. A memorial plaque to J. B. Priestley (1894–1984) states that his ashes are buried nearby. On the opposite bank of the river, across the stone bridge, is The George Inn, formerly the vicarage. It is here that the centuries-old 'Hubberholme Parliament' meets each year to auction the letting of the 'poor pasture', a 16-acre tract of rough upland behind the inn; the proceeds go to help the old people of the parish.

SKIPTON CASTLE

Just outside the southern boundary of the National Park, the busy industrial and market town of Skipton lies at an important crossroads in the Aire Gap, 22 miles north-west of Leeds. It dates from Anglo-Saxon times and is recorded in the Domesday Book as *Sceptone*, meaning 'sheep town'. The Normans built a fortress on a limestone cliff above the little Eller Beck gorge, and in the early fourteenth century the castle passed into the hands of Robert de Clifford, the 1st Lord Clifford, who rebuilt it. After a three-year siege, the castle was captured by the Parliamentarians in 1645. It was not until some five years later that Lady Anne Clifford was able to return to the severely damaged building and begin extensive restorations which continued until her death in 1675. Although in private hands, the medieval castle is open to the public and is considered to be one of the best-preserved in England.

CHAMBER END FOLD GRASSINGTON

With its cobbled market square, narrow streets and old miners' houses, Grassington is the 'capital' of Upper Wharfedale. Although there is evidence of Bronze and Iron Age occupation on the surrounding fells, the village was first settled around the eighth century by the Anglo-Saxons, at a time when dense forest cloaked Wharfedale. Towards the end of the eighteenth century the Dukes of Devonshire, the manorial owners, made substantial investments in the lead-mining industry – extracting ore on a large scale from Grassington Moor. The town prospered on mining, and also textiles, until the late nineteenth century when the industry declined. Many of the streets in the village are known as 'folds', and were created when new houses were built on the gardens of the old. Chamber End Fold, sometimes called King Street, contains houses formerly occupied by lead-miners. At the top of the narrow street is the Town Hall and Devonshire Institute, built in 1855. The town contains a National Park Information Office.

THE STRID NEAR BOLTON ABBEY

In the woods, some 2 miles upstream from Bolton Abbey, the River Wharfe rushes through a narrow millstone grit channel, known as The Strid. Its name is derived from *stride*, or possibly *stryth*, meaning 'a tumultuous force of water'. Although it is only some 4 feet wide at its narrowest, the channel is over 30 feet deep and, in attempting to leap across, many people have lost their lives. One of those said to have died while jumping The Strid was William of Egremond, the son of Alice de Romille, daughter of the founder of Embsay Priory. It is traditionally held that his mother endowed Bolton Priory in her son's memory, despite the fact that William's signature appears on the document which allowed the Augustinian canons at Embsay to move to Bolton in 1154. The Strid Woods, covering some 130 acres, are privately owned by the Trustees of the Chatsworth Settlement, a trust set up by the Duke of Devonshire.

ST MICHAEL AND ALL ANGELS' CHURCH LINTON-IN-CRAVEN

The ancient village of Linton-in-Craven is located in Wharfedale, on the south side of the river, opposite Grassington and a short distance south-east of Threshfield. It stands at the eastern boundary of the Craven district and consists of a pleasant, tree-shaded green, bordered by grey-stone houses and the almshouses of Fountaine's Hospital, founded by Richard Fountaine in 1721. The Linton Beck, which runs through the green, is crossed by a clapper-bridge, a packhorse bridge, a road bridge and a ford. Almost one mile north-east of the village, on the west bank of the River Wharfe, is Linton Church, serving the communities of a wide area, including Grassington and Threshfield. Dating from the mid-twelfth century, the long, low church has a small bell-turret instead of a tower. Stepping-stones nearby can be used to cross the river when the water level is not too high. Upstream, Linton Falls tumble over a drop in the river bed, created by the North Craven Fault.

KETTLEWELL
UPPER WHARFEDALE

Below the limestone cliffs of Middlesmoor Pasture, in the valley of the River Wharfe, the ancient village of Kettlewell is a popular tourist centre with grey-stone cottages and houses, three inns (King's Head, Bluebell and Racehorses) and a Youth Hostel. It once stood on the edge of the forests of Langstrothdale and Littondale and, in consequence, flourished as a market centre. From the twelfth century part of the manor belonged to the Premonstratensian canons of Coverham Abbey. Although it declined in the early seventeenth century, when disafforestation took place, Kettlewell was later revitalized by the textile and lead-mining industries. The church of St Mary – containing its original Norman font with the Percy crest – was rebuilt in 1820 and restored in 1882–5. A steep winding road climbs north-east out of the village to Park Rash and Tor Dyke before descending into Coverdale and Middleham.

KILNSEY CRAG
KILNSEY

Towering 170 feet above the village of Kilnsey in Wharfedale – some 4 miles upstream from Grassington – is Kilnsey Crag, an enormous cliff of Great Scar Limestone. It is often worked by rock-climbers and, because of its 40-foot overhang, is considered to be one of the most challenging climbs in the Dales. The overhang was created during the Ice Age, when the base of the cliff was cut away by the grinding action of the Wharfedale glacier. The flat fields beneath the crag once formed the bed of a huge meltwater lake. Kilnsey village, with its few houses, 'Old Hall' and inn, was once the site of a grange, or granary, owned by the monks of Fountains Abbey. The attractions of nearby Kilnsey Park include: Daleslife Visitor Centre; Trout Farm with viewing and feeding areas; fly-fishing; farm shop; picnic area; and Pony Trekking Centre. The Kilnsey Show is held annually on August Bank Holiday Tuesday.

WHARFEDALE

from Little Hunters Sleets

A cairn near Little Hunters Sleets, at the head of Park Gill Beck, provides a panoramic view south over Middle Piece Pasture to Wharfedale. Rising on the steep slopes of Oughtershaw Side, the headwaters of the River Wharfe form the Oughtershaw Beck before flowing south-east to receive the waters of the Green Field Beck near Beckermonds. Flowing past the Langstrothdale hamlets of Deepdale, Yockenthwaite and Hubberholme, the river enters Wharfedale proper to meander through lush green meadows to Buckden, Starbotton and Kettlewell. Meeting the waters of Littondale's River Skirfare near Kilnsey Crag, the Wharfe continues its southerly journey passing Threshfield, Grassington, Linton, Burnsall and Appletreewick. Before leaving the National Park, the river is squeezed through The Strid, some 2 miles upstream of Bolton Abbey. From Addingham it flows in a westerly direction, through Ilkley, Otley, Wetherby and Tadcaster to join the River Ouse near Cawood, 9 miles south of York.

YEW COGAR SCAR NEAR ARNCLIFFE

Set amidst Great Scar Limestone country, the village of Arncliffe lies in the heart of Littondale, some 2 miles south-east of Litton. It is located, among trees, on the south side of the River Skirfare, at the point where the river is joined by the Cowside Beck. Centred around a spacious green, Arncliffe contains an attractive assortment of farmhouses, cottages and barns, including The Falcon Inn, tea rooms and a post office. A local-style stone barn, with a porched entrance, is dated 1677. The Church of St Oswald, on the banks of the river, dates from the twelfth century. The photograph was taken from the road above the deep, narrow valley of the Cowside Beck, looking east across the beck to Yew Cogar Scar. The distant valley is Littondale, below Hawkswick Moor. Arncliffe lies to the left, just out of shot. The Monk's Road, an ancient monastic route from Arncliffe to Malham runs along one of the broad limestone ledges of the scar.

LITTONDALE

from Hesleden Bergh

Flanked by the long, crumbling limestone scars of the surrounding fells, the glacially formed valley of Littondale – with its barns (many with porches and double doors), level green fields and upland pastures – opens to the west of Wharfedale, one mile north of Kilnsey Crag. Rising on the slopes of Pen-y-ghent, the trout-frequented River Skirfare flows south-east down the 7-mile-long valley to the Ure, passing the farming settlements of Halton Gill, Litton, Arncliffe and Hawkswick, each about 2 miles apart. During Norman times the valley was a hunting forest, becoming, until the Dissolution, a sheep-rearing estate of Fountains Abbey. Charles Kingsley stayed for a time at Bridge End in Arncliffe, setting part of his novel *The Water Babies* in the valley, which he called 'Vendale'. Wordsworth called it 'Amerdale', and ITV chose it originally as the setting for their television series *Emmerdale Farm*. The photograph, looking down the valley towards Litton, is taken from Hesleden Bergh.

ST MICHAEL'S CHURCH KIRKBY MALHAM

Nestling in the wooded valley of the Kirkby Beck, the village of Kirkby Malham lies just over one mile south of Malham in Upper Airedale (sometimes called Malhamdale). The name 'Kirkby' suggests that the village was a former Danish settlement with a church. The present Church of St Michael the Archangel, built of millstone grit, dates from the twelfth century. Further additions and improvements were carried out over the centuries, including the addition of the 60-foot-high tower, dating from about 1490. The eleventh-century font was removed, probably during the Reformation and, after being discovered in a rubbish-heap in 1879, it was re-installed in the baptistry. Outside in the churchyard is an ancient preaching-cross. A tall, slender white-marble cross marks 'The Watery Grave', where the Harrisons are buried. It was Mrs Harrison's intention that – separated from her husband by water in life (he spent much time overseas) – they should be separated by water in death. A small stream runs through the grave plot.

MALHAM TARN
NEAR MALHAM

One of only two natural lakes in the Dales (the other being Semer Water), Malham Tarn is situated high on the moors between Wharfedale and Ribblesdale, some 2 miles north of Malham. Although in the heart of limestone country, the tarn rests on a bed of impervious Silurian slate – brought near the surface by the geological upheaval of the North Craven Fault – and also boulder clay. It was formed when the valley was blocked by a glacial moraine and is 1,229 feet above sea level, roughly half-a-mile square and 14 feet deep. Being the highest lime-rich lake of its size in England, the tarn is of particular scientific importance. The former shooting-lodge of Tarn House, standing in woods on the north shore, belongs to the National Trust and is leased to the Field Studies Council. It was largely rebuilt in about 1852 by Walter Morrison, a wealthy industrialist, whose guests included Charles Darwin, John Ruskin, Thomas Hughes and Charles Kingsley.

MALHAM COVE
MALHAM

Topped by a limestone pavement, the curved limestone crag of Malham Cove – nearly 1,000 feet wide – lies on the Mid-Craven Fault, less than a mile north of Malham. It was formed millions of years ago by a massive upheaval in the earth's crust, which caused the rock to fracture, slip and drop vertically to reveal the 300-foot-high cliff face. At one time water cascaded over the vertical cliff, creating a massive fall higher than Niagara. The stream which emerges from the crack at the base of the cliff comes from a sink on the moors near Smelt Mill Chimney, to the north-west. It is not, as is often thought, the source of the River Aire, which rises at Malham Tarn to disappear at Water Sinks before re-emerging at Aire Head Springs, just south of Malham. Centred around a small green, the ancient village of Malham is a popular centre for exploring the region. It contains two inns (one dated 1723), guest-houses, a Youth Hostel and a National Park Information Centre.

Sedbergh
and the Western Dales

RIBBLEHEAD VIADUCT
BATTY MOSS

The Ribblehead Viaduct carries the 72-mile-long Settle-to-Carlisle railway across Batty Moss. Built of local limestone, the viaduct is a quarter-of-a-mile long and contains twenty-four arches, the highest of which soars 105 feet above the surrounding moorland. After crossing the viaduct the railway line enters the Blea Moor tunnel before re-emerging into the open at the head of Dentdale. Completed in 1875, the tunnel is 2,629 yards long and reaches a maximum depth of some 500 feet. The workers and their families lived in shanty-towns in the vicinity. There are many anecdotes about the severity of the weather at Ribblehead. One story tells of a man who was blown off one side of the viaduct, through an arch, and back on to the other side. The Dales Way – an 81-mile-long footpath from Ilkley in Wharfedale to Bowness-on-Windermere – runs past the viaduct, which is now scheduled as an ancient monument.

All the main rivers in the Yorkshire Dales rise on the north-south watershed of the Pennines, or Pennine Chain – the flat-topped, rather than sharply ridged, backbone of northern England. The name 'Pennine' is derived from *Alpes Penina* and was invented by an English teacher, Charles Bertram (1723–65), who allegedly discovered and translated a fourteenth-century historical manuscript written by a monk of Westminster Abbey, Richard of Cirencester. By the time it was established that the document was a clever forgery, the name had long been accepted. Seldom rising above 2,200 feet, this broad range of hills is essentially high, wild moorland, dominated by three renowned peaks: Ingleborough (2,373 feet), Whernside (2,419 feet) and Pen-y-ghent (2,273 feet).

The Ribble rises on the north-eastern slopes of Ingleborough to flow south down Ribblesdale before turning westward to enter the Irish Sea near Preston. From its source on the Howgill Fells, the Lune also drains south, to enter the Irish Sea near Lancaster. Although the Eden and the Ure rise within half a mile of each other on Abbotside Common, the Eden flows north to Carlisle and the Solway Firth, while the Ure flows east, down Wensleydale, to the Vale of York. Like the Ure, the other four main rivers – the Aire, the Wharfe, the Nidd and the Swale – all flow eastward to join the Ouse and, eventually, the Humber before debouching into the North Sea.

Many of the dales (from the Old Norse *dalr* meaning valley) are named after their principal river: Ribblesdale (meaning 'valley of the tearing one', from the scouring action of the water); Airedale (possibly 'valley of the sacred or great one'); Nidderdale (something like the 'valley of the bright or shining one'); Wharfedale ('valley of the winding one'); and Swaledale (possibly 'valley of the rushing or swirling one'). Wensleydale, however, takes its name from the village of Wensley ('Waendel's forest clearing') and not from the River Ure.

The main road routes into and out of the Dales follow the courses of the river valleys and, as a rule, only climb up on to the high fells in order to cross from one dale-head to another. From the Vales of Mowbray and York there are three main entrances into the region: from Pateley Bridge through Greenhow Hill into Wharfedale; from Leyburn into Wensleydale; and from Richmond – the 'eastern gateway to the Dales' – into Swaledale. From Skipton – the 'southern gateway' – there are alternative routes north into Wharfe-

143

dale and north-west through Settle into Ribblesdale. One of the two westerly routes is along the old Roman Road through Ingleton to Ribble Head. The main 'western gateway', however, is the market town of Sedbergh situated near the junctions of the rivers Rawthey, Dee and Clough. Before fanning south, all roads from the north converge at Kirkby Stephen, a busy market town lying at the foot of Mallerstang fells and on the western side of the Eden Valley.

The only railway through the Dales is the Settle-to-Carlisle line, built between 1869 and 1875 to provide a new alternative service between London and Scotland. Its construction was a herculean feat of Victorian civil engineering, involving, for example, the excavation of a 2,629-yard-long tunnel under Blea Moor and the erection of a massive stone viaduct of twenty-four arches across Batty Moss. From the market town of Settle the line climbs north through Ribblesdale to Ribblehead, where it spans the dale-head at Batty Moss to enter Little Dale and, eventually, the Bleamoor Tunnel. After its re-emergence into the open, the line crosses the head of Dentdale by another viaduct and, some 3 miles further north, enters the Risehill Tunnel through which it passes into Garsdale. Beyond Garsdale Head, the line traverses White Birks Common to begin its long descent down the Valley of the Eden (with a westerly diversion through Crosby Garrett) to Appleby-in-Westmorland and eventually Carlisle.

Although, in the past, there were other passenger railways into the Dales (notably from Northallerton through Wensleydale to Garsdale Head), the Settle-to-Carlisle line is the only one not to have been closed. It passes through some of the most dramatic and spectacular countryside in England, and its opening in May 1876 brought an influx of Victorian tourists to the area. Suddenly the Dales were accessible not only to the rich, but also to the poorer classes of the newly industrialized cities. With the mass-production of motor-vehicles the following century, the influx became an invasion. Today millions of tourists and day-trippers converge on the region each and every year.

To balance the often opposing needs of visitors, conservationists, industrialists and the local community is not easy. But with careful thought and increased public awareness of environmental issues, the survival of the people and landscape of this unique and beautiful region will long be assured.

PENDRAGON CASTLE
MALLERSTANG

According to local legend, Mallerstang was the home of Uther Pendragon and the place where his son, King Arthur was born. Even now, in some undiscovered cave in the wild and craggy hills, it is said that the Knights lie sleeping, waiting until such time as England is threatened and needs their help. The crumbling remains of Pendragon Castle, however, have no connection with Arthur or his father. The fortress, on the west side of the River Eden, was first built by the Normans to guard the north-south route through the Eden or Mallerstang Valley. It was sacked by the Scots in 1341 and again in 1541. Although it was rebuilt in 1660 by Lady Anne Clifford, who owned a number of fortresses in the area, the castle fell into ruin after her death. Four miles north, standing at the meeting-point of six main routes, is the old market town of Kirkby Stephen.

ST ANDREW'S CHURCH SEDBERGH

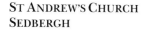

Standing at the southern foot of the Howgill Fells – above the valley of the River Rawthey and just inside the National Park boundary – the small market town of Sedbergh is the main western gateway to the Dales. It was recorded in the Domesday Book as 'Sedbergt': from the Old Norse meaning 'a flat-topped hill'. Garsdale, Dentdale and Rawthey valley all converge on this ancient settlement, which was once – like Dent – the centre of the local, domestic hand-knitting trade. During the eighteenth century cotton-spinning mills were established at Birks, Howgill and Millthrop, with a woollen mill at Hebblethwaite Hall. The Church of Saint Andrew dates from the eleventh century and was substantially restored in 1886. The Quaker Meeting House at Brigflatts, south-west of the town, was built in 1675 and is one of the oldest in England. Sedbergh School, founded in 1525 by Roger Lupton, was refounded as a free grammar school in 1552, was rebuilt in 1716 and became a public school in 1874.

DENT DENTDALE

In the heart of Dentdale, some 4 miles south-east of Sedbergh, the small township of Dent with its stone houses (many whitewashed) and narrow cobbled streets was once a 'Statesmen's' village, whose affairs were run by twenty-four Statesmen or yeoman-farmers. Today it is a popular centre for walkers and contains a post office, inns, a 'Reading Room' (dated 1880), shops and numerous guest-houses. The Church of St Andrew, part of its floor paved with Dent Marble, has a blocked Norman doorway. Near the entrance to the churchyard – in the main street – is a great slab of rough-hewn Shap granite which commemorates Adam Sedgwick, a local man who became Professor of Geology at Cambridge. A stream of water flows out of the centre of the rock into a trough. Until the close of the nineteenth century, the valley was famous for hand-knitted garments. Everyone knitted, even the children, and the community's output was so fast and furious that Robert Southey, one of the Lake Poets described them as the 'Terrible Knitters of Dent'.

DEEPDALE AND DENTDALE

from Deepdale Head

Deepdale, a tributary valley of Dentdale, is dominated by the soaring heights of Whernside (2,419 feet) and Great Coum (2,250 feet). Many of the fields in the steep-sided valley – rich in trees, pastures and farms – are separated by hedgerows rather than the usual dry-stone walls. Deepdale Beck, rising on the western slopes of Whernside, flows north down the valley to Dentdale, where it joins the River Dee before eventually merging with the Lune near Sedbergh. The Dent Fault (dividing Dentdale into two separate geological zones) crosses the valley near Gawthrop, less than a mile west of Dent. In Dentdale, the change between the two different types of rocks (Silurian slates and Carboniferous limestones and sandstones) can be clearly seen at Combe Scar. The narrow moorland road south from Deepdale climbs over the 1,552-foot-high summit of White Shaw Moss before descending into Kingsdale and Ingleton.

DENT HEAD VIADUCT

The building of the Settle-to-Carlisle line was one of the great engineering feats of the Railway Age. It took more than 5,000 men six years to complete and hundreds of labourers lost their lives during its construction. The line was first opened to goods traffic in 1875 and to passenger trains the following year. The Dent Head viaduct, north of Blea Moor, has ten arches, is 596 feet long and reaches a maximum height of 100 feet. Just over a mile north of the viaduct is a small tributary valley of the River Dee. This is crossed by the Arten Gill viaduct: 660 feet long, with eleven arches and a maximum height of 117 feet. It is built of a dark, highly fossilized limestone of local origin, known as 'Dent Marble'. During Victorian times this stone – cut and finished in Dentdale factories – was in vogue for fireplaces, ornaments and tables. Dent Station, at 1,150 feet above sea level, is the highest main-line station in England.

INGLEBOROUGH

from Souther Scales Fell

At 2,373 feet above sea level, Ingleborough is the second highest peak in Yorkshire – its square flat-topped bulk dominating the limestone landscape for miles around. Capped by a 100-foot-thick slab of millstone grit (resting on 1,000 feet of shales and sandstones, below which is a 600-foot-thick bed of limestone), the mountain, as well as the surrounding hills and dales, is riddled with caves and potholes. Gaping Gill, on its south-eastern flank, is the most famous pothole in Britain. A stream (Fell Beck) flows over its roughly circular limestone mouth to plunge 340 feet into a gigantic cavern large enough to contain the nave of York Minster. The water which enters the underground system re-emerges into the open near the entrance to Ingleborough Cave, one of three show caves within the National Park. It was first opened to the public in 1837. The summit, once the site of a 15-acre Iron Age fort, can be reached from Clapham, Ingleton, Chapel-le-Dale and Selside.

NORBER BOULDERS
NEAR AUSTWICK

On the south-eastern flanks of Ingleborough, at Norber Brow, over 500 feet above Austwick, the sloping limestone plateau is strewn with hundreds of 'erratics'. These giant boulders, composed of dark grey Silurian slate and each weighing several tons, are perched on low pedestals of white limestone. For centuries the reason for their alien presence in the landscape was unexplained, for Silurian slate is usually found beneath Carboniferous limestone rather than on it. It is now known that the boulders were transported from Crummack Dale, about half-a-mile away, by a glacier during the last Ice Age. The explanation for the fact that many of the 'erratics' are perched on plinths, some a foot high, is that the surrounding softer limestone – unprotected by the umbrella effect of the harder boulders – has been dissolved away by 10,000 years of rainfall. They can be reached by an easy climb of less than a mile from the former Viking settlement of Austwick.

CLAPHAM

Now by-passed by the busy Settle-to-Ingleton main road, the estate village of Clapham nestles in a wooded valley at the south-eastern foot of Ingleborough. The little Clapham Beck, spanned by no fewer than four bridges, flows through the centre of the village, which contains a mainly Victorian church, a National Park Information Office, a school and a post office. It is one of the few villages still without street lighting. Ingleborough Hall, now an outdoor education centre, was once the home of Reginald Farrer (1880–1920), the 'Father of English rock gardening', who introduced many rare exotic plants to Britain. A 'Reginald Farrer Nature Trail' leads from the village, through the Ingleborough Estate (containing a lake created by damming the beck) to the mouth of Ingleborough Cave. Michael Faraday (1791–1867), discoverer of electro-magnetism, was the son of the village blacksmith. The popular monthly magazine *The Dalesman* (originally *The Yorkshire Dalesman*) was founded at Clapham in 1939 and is still published in the village.

ST ALKELDA'S CHURCH GIGGLESWICK

Less than a mile west of Settle, just outside the boundary of the National Park, is the ancient Pennine village of Giggleswick. The church dates from the twelfth century and is dedicated to Alkelda, a tenth-century saint about whom very little is known. Legend says that she was a Saxon, living in Yorkshire, who was strangled by the Danes because of her faith. The famous public school, with its green-domed chapel, was founded in 1507 by James Carr. To the north of the village, the line of the South Craven Fault can be clearly seen at Giggleswick Scar. A large cairn above the lime quarry, known as 'Schoolboys Tower', was built by boys from Giggleswick School. The water in a well by the roadside on Buck Haw Brow is reputed to rise and fall because of an underground siphon in the rocks below; hence its name, the Ebbing and Flowing Well.

THORNTON FORCE INGLETON

The Ingleton Waterfalls Trail, first opened to the public in 1885, runs up the valley of the River Doe from Ingleton, crosses the open moor below Twisleton Scar, and returns down the valley of the River Twiss. (There is some confusion, however, about these two river names, for they are transposed on Ordnance Survey maps and also in the Falls guide). The 4-mile trail is of particular importance to geologists for it reveals the ancient basement rocks of the Pennines, crosses three major faults, and – at Thornton Force – presents a classic example of an 'unconformity': an abrupt change or break between rocks of a vastly different age, defined by a sharp boundary line. At Thornton Force the 'unconformity' separates the upper horizontal layers of younger Carboniferous limestone from the lower almost vertical layers of older Ordovician slate. Here, it has been said, the breadth of a hand can span 300 million years. With a drop of 46 feet, the fall is the highest of the Ingleton waterfalls.

PHOTOGRAPHER'S NOTES

I was introduced to Yorkshire many years ago and have been a regular tourist/visitor ever since. It is a region of such great contrasts: the Coast; the Moors; the Dales; the limestone pavements; the steep-sided valleys; the ever-changing colours of the moorland; and the unpredictable moods of the sea. Things to do, places to visit, to be as busy or as quiet as you like.

As a photographer I tend to work alone, rising early, working late and taking an eternity over each shot, and then, moving on to, or planning for, the next one. For companionship I have a faithful border collie, who seems quite happy to wait hours or walk miles. He is very patient, and a good listener too.

The quantity of equipment I use is fairly extensive, but I always select the smallest amount possible for a particular shoot so as to keep the weight and choices to a minimum. I very much enjoy working on 35mm equipment, the versatility and flexibility being unequalled. The quality attainable is quite superb. Strangely, however, I still find myself mostly working with a heavy medium-format camera for the simple reason that the resulting transparency is many times larger and, therefore, easier to see. This is appreciated by designers, art directors, editors, and those who frequently view transparencies. The quality difference between the two formats, on book-sized enlargements, is practically indiscernible.

Good photography, however, really comes down to good technique – and then a certain determination to do the best you can!

I have always greatly admired the work of Frank Meadow Sutcliffe, the Victorian photographer who based much of his work on the people and landscapes surrounding and including Whitby. But I became an even greater fan as to some extent I retraced his footsteps. Incredibly, through his heavy and cumbersome wooden camera and without the convenience of gelatine film, he was able to record images perfect in their composition and delicate in their lighting: pictures both elegant and sensitive, yet images that truly captured a special moment.

It is useful to reflect – while using modern photographic equipment and film stocks, and while travelling in the comfort of cars – on the time and sheer effort pioneer photographers like Sutcliffe must have made to take such memorable pictures. Perhaps, we photographers should all try a little harder? What could be more rewarding than to capture a fleeting moment of today for those who bear witness to tomorrow?

Rob Talbot

SELECTED PROPERTIES

ENGLISH HERITAGE

All English Heritage properties, except where specified, are open from April to end September (10am–6pm) and from October to March, Tuesday–Sunday (10am–4pm), and are closed on 24, 25 and 26 December and 1 January.

North Region Properties in Care
Bessie Surtees House, 41/44 Sandhill, Newcastle-upon-Tyne NE1 3JF
Tel: (091) 2611585

Aldborough Roman Town
Aldborough, near Boroughbridge YO2 3PH
Open: April to end September; October to March, grounds only (admission free)
Closed: 24–26 December & 1 January
Tel: (09012) 2768

Byland Abbey
near Coxwold YO6 4BD
Open: April to end September (10am–6pm); October to Maundy Thursday (10am–4pm)
Closed: Mondays, 24–26 December & 1 January
Tel: (03476) 614

Clifford's Tower
Tower Street, York YO1 1SA
Open: Throughout the year, except 24–26 December & 1 January
Tel: (0904) 646940

Easby Abbey
Easby, near Richmond, North Yorkshire

Gisborough Priory
Church Street, Guisborough TS14 6HL
Tel: (0287) 638301

Helmsley Castle
Helmsley, North Yorkshire
Tel: (0439) 70442

Kirkham Priory
Whitwell-on-the-Hill, York YO6 7JS
Tel: (065381) 768

Middleham Castle
Middleham, Leyburn, North Yorkshire
Tel: (0969) 23899

Mount Grace Priory
Osmotherly, Northallerton DL6 3JG
Tel: (0609) 83494

Pickering Castle
Pickering, North Yorkshire
Tel: (0751) 74989

Richmond Castle
Richmond DL10 4QW
Tel: (0748) 2493

Rievaulx Abbey
Rievaulx, Helmsley YO6 5LB
Tel: (04396) 228

Scarborough Castle
Castle Road, Scarborough YO1 1HY
Tel: (0723) 372451

Whitby Abbey
Whitby, North Yorkshire
Tel: (0947) 603568

NATIONAL TRUST

Regional Office
The National Trust, Goddards, 27 Tadcaster Road, Dringhouses, York YO2 2QG
Tel: (0904) 702021

Fountains Abbey & Studley Royal
Fountains, Ripon HG4 3DZ
Open: Abbey & Gardens all year, except Christmas & Fridays from November to January; Deer Park open all year.
Tel: (076586) 639

Rievaulx Terrace & Temples
Rievaulx, Helmsley YO6 5LJ
Open: Easter to end October
Tel: (04396) 340

MISCELLANEOUS

Bolton Castle
Castle Bolton, Leyburn DL8 4ET
Open: March to end October; November to March tours by special arrangement
Tel: (0969) 23981/23674

Bolton Priory
Estate Office, Bolton Abbey, Skipton BD23 6EX
Open: Throughout the year
Tel: (075671) 227

Castle Howard
York YO6 7DA
Open: Easter to end October
Tel: (065384) 333

Kilnsey Park
Kilnsey, Near Skipton BD23 5PS
Open: Throughout the year
Tel: (0756) 752150 or 752861 for pony trekking

Newburgh Priory
Coxwold, York YO6 4AS
Open: May to end August, Wednesdays and Sundays, Easter Monday and August Bank Holiday Monday
Tel: (03476) 435

Skipton Castle
Skipton BD23 1AQ
Open: Every day, except Christmas Day
Tel: (0756) 792442

SELECT BIBLIOGRAPHY

Bede, *The Ecclesiastical History of the English Nation*, Dent, nd

Booth, R. K., *York: The History and Heritage of a City*, Barrie & Jenkins, 1990

Brumhead, D., *Geology Explained in the Yorkshire Dales and on the Yorkshire Coast*, David & Charles, Newton Abbot, 1979

Burns, Tom Scott, & Rigg, Martin, *Round and About The North Yorkshire Moors*, M. T. D. Rigg, Leeds, 1987 (vol. I) and 1988 (vol. II)

David, Joy (ed.), *The Hidden Places of North Yorkshire*, Maps Marketing, Plymouth, 1989

Dykes, Jack, *Yorkshire's Whaling Days*, Dalesman, Clapham, 1980

Fawcett, Edward R., *Lead Mining in Swaledale*, Faust, Burnley, 1985

Fletcher, J. S., *A Picturesque History of Yorkshire* (3 Vols.), Dent, 1900

Godfrey, Arthur, & Lassey, Peter J., *Shipwrecks of the Yorkshire Coast*, Dalesman, Clapham, 1989

Gunn, Peter, *The Yorkshire Dales*, Century, 1984

Harding, Mike, *Walking the Dales*, Michael Joseph, 1986

Hartley, Marie, & Ingilby, Joan, *Life & Traditions in the Moorlands of North-East Yorkshire*, Dent, 1972

Hartley, Marie, & Ingilby, Joan, *Life & Traditions in the Yorkshire Dales*, Dalesman, Clapham, 1989

Hayes, Raymond H., *A History of Rosedale*, North York Moors National Park, Helmsley, 1985

Hayes, Raymond H., *Old Roads & Pannierways in North East Yorkshire*, North York Moors National Park, Helmsley, 1988

Hayes, R. H., & Rutter, J. G., *Rosedale Mines & Railway* (Research Report No. 9), Archaeological & Historical Society, Scarborough, 1974

Hayes, R. H., & Rutter, J. G., *Wade's Causeway* (Research Report No. 4), Archaeological & Historical Society, Scarborough, 1964

Herriot, James, *James Herriot's Yorkshire*, Michael Joseph, 1979

Heselden, Jean & Snelling, Rebecca (eds.), *North York Moors*, Automobile Association & Ordnance Survey Basingstoke, 1987

Houses of the North York Moors, H.M.S.O., 1987

Joy, David, *Steam on the North York Moors*, Dalesman, Clapham, 1986

Mee, Arthur, *Yorkshire East Riding with York* (The King's England series), Hodder and Stoughton, 1941

Mee, Arthur, *Yorkshire North Riding* (The King's England series), Hodder and Stoughton, 1941

Mee, Arthur, *Yorkshire West Riding* (The King's England series), Hodder and Stoughton, 1941

Mitchell, W. R., *Exploring the Captain Cook Country*, Dalesman, Clapham, 1978

Mitchell, W. R., & Joy, David, *Settle to Carlisle: A Railway over the Pennines*, Dalesman, Clapham, 1989

Mitchell, W. R., & Fox, Peter, *The Story of Ribblehead Viaduct*, Castleberg, Giggleswick, 1990

Morris, John (ed.), *Domesday Book: Yorkshire* (Pts. I & II), Phillimore, Chichester, 1986

Parker, Malcolm, & Grant, Pamela, *Historic City of York*, Discovery Guides, Durham, 1988

Parker, Malcolm, & Hillery, Caroline, *North York Moors & Coast*, Discovery Guides, Durham, 1988

Parker, Malcolm, & Lind-Jackson, Celia, *The Yorkshire Dales*, Discovery Guides, Durham, 1988

Pevsner, Nikolaus, *Yorkshire North Riding* (Buildings of England series), Penguin, 1966

Pevsner, Nikolaus, *Yorkshire West Riding* (Buildings of England series), Penguin, 1959

Pevsner, Nikolaus, *Yorkshire: York & The East Riding* (Buildings of England series), Penguin, 1972

Raistrick, Arthur (ed.), *North York Moors: National Park Guide No. 4*, H.M.S.O., 1969

Raistrick, Arthur, *Old Yorkshire Dales*, David & Charles, Newton Abbot, 1968

Raistrick, Arthur, *The Pennine Dales*, Eyre & Spottiswoode, 1968

Raistrick, Arthur, *Vikings, Angles & Danes in Yorkshire*, Dalesman, Clapham, 1965

Sampson, Ian, *Cleveland Way* (National Trail Guide: 3), Aurum Press, 1989

Scott, Harry J., *Portrait of Yorkshire*, Robert Hale, 1965

Simmons, I. G., *Yorkshire Dales National Park*, H.M.S.O., 1971

Spence, Joan & Bill, *Romantic Ryedale*, Ambo, Helmsley, 1977

Spencer, Brian, *Visitor's Guide to Yorkshire Dales & North Pennines*, Moorland Publishing, Ashbourne, 1990

Spratt, D. A., & Harrison, B. J. D. (eds.), *The North York Moors Landscape Heritage*, David & Charles, Newton Abbot, 1989

Staniforth, Alan, *Geology of the North York Moors*, North York Moors National Park, Helmsley, 1990

Wainwright, A., *A Coast to Coast Walk*, Westmorland Gazette, Kendal, 1973

Wainwright, A., *Pennine Way Companion*, Westmorland Gazette, Kendal, 1968

Wainwright, A., *Walks in Limestone Country*, Westmorland Gazette, Kendal, 1970

White, Stanhope, *Standing Stones & Earthworks on the North Yorkshire Moors*, White, Scarborough, 1987

Wood, Donna (ed.), *Yorkshire Dales*, Automobile Association & Ordnance Survey, Basingstoke, 1985

Wright, Geoffrey N., *Roads & Trackways of The Yorkshire Dales*, Moorland, Ashbourne, 1985

Wright, Geoffrey N., *The Yorkshire Dales*, David & Charles, Newton Abbot, 1986

INDEX

Page numbers in *italics* denote photographs.